THE YES BRAIN
WORKBOOK

DANIEL J. SIEGEL, M.D.
TINA PAYNE BRYSON, Ph.D.

Copyright © 2020 Daniel J. Siegel and Tina Payne Bryson

Published by
PESI Publishing & Media
PESI, Inc.
3839 White Ave
Eau Claire, WI 54703

Cover: Misa Erder & Amy Rubenzer
Editing: Bookmasters
Layout: Amy Rubenzer & Bookmasters
Illustrations: Tuesday Mourning

ISBN: 9781683732976

PESI
Publishing
& Media
pesipublishing.com

Table of Contents

CHAPTER 1

Introduction

The Yes Brain ... allows a person to feel grounded and understand themselves,
to flexibly learn and adapt, and to live with a sense of purpose. It leads them
not only to survive difficult situations, but to emerge from them stronger and wiser.

—The Yes Brain

In today's world it can feel like there are an infinite number of experiences that cause us stress. Just making it through the day can feel overwhelming at times. For our children, whose brains are still developing and who have less life experience than we do, this is especially true. Daily interactions that seem simple to us can cause them to unravel. However, by encouraging kids to develop a Yes Brain, we can help them better navigate their world such that their experiences become opportunities for growth and learning.

WHAT'S A YES BRAIN?

As we explain in our book *The Yes Brain*, parenting from a Yes Brain perspective isn't about being permissive or telling our kids yes all the time. Nor is it about clearing the path so that everything's easy for them. Instead, it's about helping them develop an approach to the world that allows them to tackle the challenges they'll face in a flexible, receptive, open-minded manner. A Yes Brain mindset allows children to better understand their own emotions and physical responses so they are actively *responding* to events, not automatically *reacting* to them. In doing this, instead of being thrown off course, they expand their "window of tolerance" for adversity and can adapt when hit with the setbacks that are an inherent part of life.

WHAT A YES BRAIN LOOKS LIKE

When kids approach the world with a Yes Brain, they're operating from the upper parts of their brain, specifically from the part associated with executive functioning. A child with more well-developed executive functioning will have an easier time being flexible and resilient when things don't go her or his way.

WHAT'S A NO BRAIN?

A No Brain, on the other hand, emerges more from the lower, more primitive regions of the brain. Children stuck in their No Brain tend to see the world as a place full of competition and threat, and therefore respond with stubbornness, anxiety, and defensiveness when faced with setbacks. This mindset leaves them much less capable of handling difficult situations or understanding themselves and others.

WHAT A NO BRAIN LOOKS LIKE

The problem with a No Brain state is that it is highly reactive and keeps kids from being in control of their own emotions, bodies, and decisions. They're at the mercy of their circumstances, doomed to simply react to whatever happens to them, rather than intentionally deciding who they want to be and how they want to act and behave.

Children who approach their world from this No Brain state of mind often get stuck in their emotions, unable to move beyond their upset to find a more adaptive way of responding. Generally, younger children operate from this perspective more often than older ones, but everyone (even parents) can get stuck in their No Brain!

IMAGINE THE DIFFERENCE

Ask yourself a question: How would life at your house change if your kids were better at responding to everyday situations from a Yes Brain instead of a No Brain? What would screen-time battles, homework struggles, conflict with siblings, or bedtime arguments look like if your child were responding with a Yes Brain?

- What if he was less rigid and stubborn and could better regulate himself when things don't go his way?
- What if she welcomed new experiences instead of fearing them?
- What if he could be more clear about his feelings, and more caring and empathic toward others?
- How much happier would she be? How much happier and more peaceful would your family be?

Let's take a minute now to write out what you imagine life could be like if your children were operating from a Yes Brain more often. There are no rules here. Just write about what might be different.

_____

_____

_____

_____

_____

_____

_____

Now that you've visualized what it could be like having children who respond from their Yes Brain more often, let's get to work helping them actually achieve that goal.

WHAT DOES IT LOOK LIKE?

Before you can help your child move from one state of mind to another, it's helpful to be able to identify what each state looks like. What signs does your child give that he's operating from a No Brain or Yes Brain state? What behaviors does she exhibit when she's becoming dysregulated and moving into a No Brain state? How can you tell when he's starting to move back into a state of equilibrium?

In the next few moments we want to give you a chance to consider your individual children and what a Yes Brain and a No Brain looks like for them. Next, you'll find a list of behaviors, actions, and expressions. After the list, we've given you two columns—one marked "Yes Brain" and one marked "No Brain." Read through the descriptive words and think about whether any of them seem familiar when you think about how your child reacts and responds to challenging situations. Does she fidget or pick a fight? Does she typically remain unbothered? Read through and see which behaviors fit your experience with your child. (By the way, most likely, you'll see in this exercise that your child often exhibits both Yes Brain and No Brain responses when they face difficulties.)

When a behavior fits, add it to the appropriate column on the next page. If you're doing this for more than one child, feel free to use a separate sheet of paper. (Note: This isn't a definitive list. If behaviors your child exhibits aren't here, go ahead and add anything that tips you off to his mental state.)

- Fidgeting
- Picking fights
- Unbothered
- Excessive sleeping
- Argumentative
- Avoidant
- Deep sighs
- Excited
- Lack of focus
- Apathetic
- Stubborn
- Panic
- Able to take in other points of view
- Upset over small things
- Confident
- Crying
- Procrastination
- Biting nails
- Change in eating
- Trouble falling/staying asleep
- Calm
- Focused
- Able to articulate their points clearly
- Flexible
- Steady breathing
- Anxious
- Sees challenges as opportunity
- Perseverant
- Upbeat
- Rigid

My Child's Yes Brain Signs　　　　　　　　　　　　**My Child's No Brain Signs**

_____　　　　_____

_____　　　　_____

_____　　　　_____

_____　　　　_____

_____　　　　_____

_____　　　　_____

_____　　　　_____

_____　　　　_____

_____　　　　_____

While it's probably no surprise to see certain unwanted behaviors in the No Brain column, what's important to recognize here is what your child's particular go-to behaviors are. When you notice the pattern that a trying situation often leads your child to bite her nails or sleep longer than usual, you can use those data points to help you notice when she's upset, and step in to help in a more proactive way (more about that later.)

Next, we're going to ask you to think about what tends to set your child off when it comes to this way of thinking. Take a look at the chart that follows.

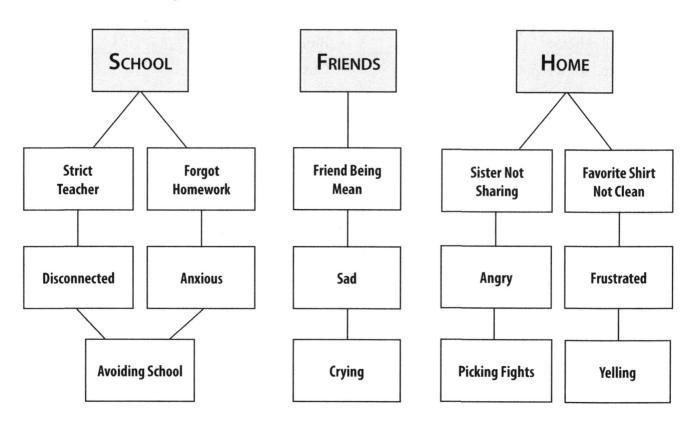

You'll see we've given you an example of what might happen in a child's typical day, and a simplified idea of what the resulting emotions and behaviors could be for a child stuck in a No Brain state.

As you can see, an average day can present a lot of challenges for a child. And for one whose brain is less integrated—meaning its various parts aren't working together as an integrated whole—the results can be unwanted behavior and more stress.

However, it's possible to help our kids learn to shift into their Yes Brain, even when faced with multiple challenges in a day. Now that you've zoomed in on your kids' specific behaviors, and thought about how challenges lead to reactive behaviors, zoom out to consider what interactions and experiences throughout the day tend to contribute to your own children slipping into a No Brain state and what you can do to help them remain in their Yes Brain.

For example, consider your children's typical week and review the list that follows. As you look through it, circle any dynamic that you think would be challenging to your kids and could result in some of those No Brain emotions and behaviors you listed earlier. We left blank spaces for you to add in anything specific that your children struggle with.

- Parental anger or reactivity
- Visiting extended family
- Change of plans
- Losing game
- Broken toy
- Uncomfortable clothing/ getting dressed
- Having to do a less preferred activity
- Bedtime
- Bath time
- Mealtime
- Personal care (brushing hair, brushing teeth, etc.)
- Siblings getting parental attention
- Going to school
- Attending new class/new teacher
- Travel
- Loss (friend, family, pet, etc.)

- Doing homework/studying
- Separating from parents
- Turning off screens
- After-school practice (musical instrument, tutor, etc.)
- Waking up
- Getting ready for school
- Not being able to do something well
- Chores
- Friendship struggles (being left out, being teased, being pressured, etc.)
- Tests
- _____
- _____
- _____
- _____
- _____
- _____

- Physical discomfort (too hot, too cold, hungry, braces hurt, feet hurt, itchy skin, scraped knee, etc.)
- Request denied
- Puberty/self-consciousness
- Being late
- Being rushed
- Transitions
- Parents fighting
- Teacher is impatient/uses them as example to whole class (shame, embarrassment, discomfort)
- Poor night's sleep
- _____
- _____
- _____
- _____
- _____
- _____

Adults are often juggling so much in their hectic lives that it's easy to forget how stressful small things can be for children. Not only do they have less experience with the world, but their not-yet-fully-developed brains are less capable of handling these challenges. But now, you've at least thought about some of the most common ways your kids express themselves when they're in a No Brain state, and the more you can see where they're coming from, the more you can offer your assistance.

So, How Can I Help?

That's really what we want to talk about for most of this workbook. As we discuss in *The Yes Brain*, our children need to learn how to access their Yes Brain state of mind when they're thrown off course. We, as parents, are the logical place where that learning stems from. Let's take a first step toward figuring out how, exactly, we can do that.

In this next exercise, take your answers from the two previous activities and place them in the appropriate columns that follow.

- In the first column, list one of the triggering events you know can cause a No Brain state for your child.
- In the second column, look through your child's corresponding No Brain behavior list that you completed previously and choose one—or more—that they would exhibit as a result of the trigger in column one.
- And finally, in the third column, consider what specific steps you can take to help your child remain in their Yes Brain the next time they're faced with a similar challenge.

This is not only about how to react to your child in the moment of their upset, but also about what tools your child needs help accessing when faced with similar circumstances. We gave you a couple of examples to start you off. Continue to fill in the chart with as many examples as you can think of.

TRIGGERING EVENT	NO BRAIN REACTION	YES BRAIN STRATEGY
Parental anger or reactivity	• Defensive • Stubborn • Crying	• *First, listen to her feelings and help her "feel felt."* • *Remind her that even parents have No Brain moments and acknowledge any Yes Brain responses she had to my upset that helped me to regulate.* • *Point out that neither of us gets what we want when we're in our No Brain state and work together on how to compromise next time.*

TRIGGERING EVENT	NO BRAIN REACTION	YES BRAIN STRATEGY
A teacher who quashes my child's creativity	• Avoidant • Apathetic	• *Listen to and reflect his feelings.* • *Role-play with him and reenact the scene while talking through his emotional response to the teacher's comments.* • *Have him help explore why the teacher may be coming from a No Brain state (anxious about finishing lesson on time, concerned about how one child veering off topic might lead others to—loss of control, etc.)* • *Together brainstorm ways to approach the project that still feel creative to him but respect the teacher's boundaries.*

Over time, and as our children develop, the ability to return to a Yes Brain state of mind will become more natural to them, and they will need our help less and less to do so. But for now, we need to continue to help them build their ability to regulate and bounce back from difficulties.

One of the best ways to do this is through integration.

THE YES BRAIN AND INTEGRATION

The brain is made up of many different parts, each having its own job to do. When these differentiated parts are also integrated and able to work together, our brains function better and can accomplish more—in terms of academics, relationships, career, and mental health. Luckily, we have so many opportunities to give the children we love the types of experiences that help develop the key characteristics of an integrated brain.

The FACES of an Integrated Brain

FLEXIBLE

ADAPTIVE

COHERENT

ENERGIZED

STABLE

A brain that's well integrated is a brain that's more flexible, adaptive, coherent, energized, and stable. Take a minute to think about how your child responds to the world and its challenges.

- **F**lexible: Being able to shift mentally and emotionally, or to handle transitions or changes well.
- **A**daptive: Considering options and the environment, then responding in a way that elicits the best results.
- **C**oherent: Viewing the world accurately, in a way that's clear-sighted and objective to the greatest possible degree.
- **E**nergized: Remaining alert, engaged, and full of life.
- **S**table: Feeling grounded, balanced, and as though she has a steady foundation from which to respond to events.

On the chart that follows, write examples of scenarios your children might face that cause them to struggle. We've started you off with a few common situations, so you can consider your individual child and add more examples that apply. Then, in each of the FACES columns, on a 1–5 scale, with one being extreme difficulty and five being very capable, rate your child's ability to be flexible, adaptive, coherent, energized, and stable.

As you continue to work toward supporting your child's brain integration, this chart should give you a sense of which aspects are areas of strength and which he struggles most with.

EVENT	FLEXIBLE	ADAPTIVE	COHERENT	ENERGIZED	STABLE
Unexpected change of plans					
Leaving playdate to go home					
Losing a game					

READY, SET, INTEGRATE!

One of the best methods for encouraging our kids' brain integration is to provide experiences that focus their attention in positive ways. Remember, it's not just our way of thinking that changes as we grow and experience new events; the actual physical structure of our brains adapts and reorganizes based on what we see, hear, touch, think about, practice, and so on. Anything we focus on and give attention to creates new connections in our brains—a process known as neuroplasticity. In other words, where attention goes, neurons fire. And where neurons fire, they wire, or join together.

WHERE ATTENTION GOES NEURAL FIRING FLOWS and NEURAL CONNECTION GROWS

While kids can be positively influenced by their experiences, at the same time we need to be aware that neglecting aspects of a child's development can result in a lack of optimal integration. For example, when we encourage our kids to see events from someone else's point of view, we're helping them rewire their brains in a positive, Yes Brain way. Their brain is getting exercise in accessing skills such as patience, flexible thinking, and empathy. However, if over time, he's never made aware that situations can be seen from many angles, the neurons that control the various parts of his brain don't have a chance to become as well connected and, as a result, rigid, No Brain behavior is more likely to occur.

Let's tune in now to what experiences your kids are having and how you're helping them focus their minds and attention. Consider both positive and negative experiences. In the chart that follows we've given you space to list experiences and activities you give your child—a trip to the grocery store, a school day, nighttime routines, and more. Once you've listed more specifics, think critically about what your child is learning from each one (advocating for herself, flexibility, making friends, etc.) and fill in the matching "skills" section.

Next, decide whether the unspoken communication your child is receiving from that activity fits your morals and values and encourages Yes Brain thinking, or if you feel there needs to be some adjustment because the experience seems to be further entrenching No Brain thinking. Then mark off the corresponding column. Additionally, you may find that while some experiences will feel positive, there are changes you want to make that will make them even better. If that happens, you can mark off both the "Continue Experience?" *and* "Make a Change" columns.

Let's get started. As usual, we've given you a few examples to get the ball rolling.

EXPERIENCE/ACTIVITY	UNSPOKEN MESSAGE OR COMMUNICATION	CONTINUE EXPERIENCE?	MAKE A CHANGE
Mom lays out child's clothes each night	• Someone else will do for you what you really could do for yourself. • You are not responsible enough yet to handle picking out your clothes.		✓
Dad patiently encourages summer camp attendance even though the child is nervous about it	• You can handle challenges and can face your fears.	✓	
Parents keep telling him to turn off screens, but ultimately allow the child to stay up late playing video games.	• Sleep isn't a priority. • Your parents don't follow through and you don't *really* have to follow instructions until they get really mad.	✓	✓

This isn't an exercise meant to make you feel guilty about your parenting. Rather, it's an opportunity to take a good look at the big picture and think about how your kids spend their time, what's working well, and what—if anything—you'd like to improve on.

Take a minute to acknowledge how many positive interactions your kids are getting on a regular basis! You're doing a great job! And it's probably so much more than you realized. Observe, too, whether you typically provide activities that allow your child to stay calmly in her Yes Brain. As we'll discuss in future chapters, it's a delicate balance between, on one hand, knowing where your child is happy and giving her experiences that allow for it, and on the other, challenging her to step outside her comfort zone so she's more likely to get the integration workout her brain needs—like a bodybuilder only working on one set of muscles!

Taking that into consideration, in the left-hand column in the chart that follows, list only the activities you feel are not giving your child the opportunities for the brain integration you want him to have. In the middle column, write out what adjustments you'd like to make. And in the right hand column, list the skills you think he will gain from these changes.

EXPERIENCE/ACTIVITY	ADJUSTMENTS	SKILLS
Mom lays out child's clothes each night	• *Encourage him to choose his own clothes* • *Discuss with him the pros and cons of doing it the night before versus the morning of*	• Independence • Autonomy • Responsibility
Parents keep telling him to turn off screens, but ultimately allow the child to stay up late playing video games	• *Review homework schedule—make sure there is time for homework/studying to get done* • *Set and enforce time limit and bedtime* • *Consider only allowing video games on the weekend*	• Accountability • Discipline • Practice dealing with disappointment

Now that you've done that, what action statements are in order? Make yourself a short, specific "To Do" list based on this exercise. Given the adjustments you'd like to make, what do you need to do next? What support do you need to get it done?

- _____
- _____
- _____

- _____
- _____
- _____

Taking a critical look at what your child does on a regular basis isn't always comfortable for parents, but we hope this exercise has helped you see not only where there's room for improvement but also where you're doing a great job. Brain growth and integration are an ongoing experience, and it's always good to step back and review from time to time!

THE FOUR FUNDAMENTALS OF THE YES BRAIN

In our other books we've talked about the upstairs brain, the part of the brain that's in charge of practically all the behaviors we expect from a mature and caring human being with an active Yes Brain: flexibility and adaptability, sound decision making and planning, regulation of emotions and body, personal insight, empathy, and morality.

In the rest of this book we want to talk to you about these various behaviors, narrowing them down into what we call the **Four Fundamentals of the Yes Brain.**

Each of the next four chapters will focus on one of these fundamentals, exploring it in depth and talking about practical ways you can help develop that particular characteristic in your child. The more your child develops each fundamental, the closer she'll move toward displaying all the benefits that come with a Yes Brain.

- **Balance:** When your children are overwhelmed with big emotions, balance helps them know how to regulate their emotions and physical reactions, and how to continue to make good decisions even when upset. Also, balance is about having a variety of healthy activities and a schedule that promotes health and wellness.
- **Resilience:** If your child tends to fall apart when he's struggling, resilience allows him to be able to push through challenges and be persistent even in the face of setbacks.
- **Insight:** Developing the ability to understand herself and her emotions allows your child to be able to decide what she cares about and who she wants to be.
- **Empathy:** All of these skills create a strong foundation for your child to be able to understand and care for himself and others, and to act in moral and ethical ways.

On a 1–5 scale, with one being extreme difficulty and five being fully confident, circle how you would rate your child's fluency and ability to access these four life skills.

Balance	1	2	3	4	5
Resilience	1	2	3	4	5
Insight	1	2	3	4	5
Empathy	1	2	3	4	5

As you look over this chart, you'll get a sense of which fundamentals are currently easiest for your child, and which ones she needs the most help with. While some kids' temperaments lead them to be naturally more balanced, resilient, insightful, or empathic, remember that a child's brain is plastic and malleable, and there are plenty of opportunities to reinforce any areas in which they struggle.

In other words, these are skills that kids can learn! So, let's move forward and get some practice making that happen.

CHAPTER 2

Balance

All kids lose their emotional balance. It might happen more or less frequently,
but becoming dysregulated is simply par for the childhood course. Childhood is about
learning to experience a wide array of types and intensities of emotions, and that, by necessity, means
sometimes "losing control" as the intensity of emotions overwhelms the ability to think clearly.

—*The Yes Brain*

Everything we hope for our children—emotional happiness, success in school, fulfilling relationships with friends and family, even just a good night's sleep—depends on balance. Without it, you have a child who is out of control and reactive, unable to make good decisions or learn from their experiences because of their emotional dysregulation. In addition, the other three Yes Brain fundamentals—resilience, insight, and empathy—all stem from a child having a certain amount of emotional stability and regulation. In other words, balance is absolutely crucial to a child's functioning—and when big emotions hit, helping our kids regulate is often a parent's first job. After all, how can we expect them to successfully meet a challenge if they can't first manage their emotional response to it?

Because our children look to us for guidance, and because our response to them influences whether their challenging behaviors escalate or diminish, it's helpful to understand how much we contribute to that cycle. Do you respond in ways that help your kids calm down, get back into balance, and make good decisions? Or do you respond in ways that escalate their dysregulation and make it harder for them to return to balance? How often do you focus on teaching your child skills that can help them do this on their own when faced with overwhelming emotions? Do you model staying balanced emotionally most of the time, even when things get really hard? Do you have support in helping you keep your own dysregulation in check so you have a greater capacity to remain balanced even when your children are dysregulated and push your buttons?

A No Brain response further frustrates a child

A Yes Brain response calms a child and helps build skills

Let's start with looking at how you typically respond to your child when they're upset. The following chart contains two columns: On the left is a list of typical responses you might have when your child is having a hard time, along with some free space to add your own examples. On the right is space to list what percentage of the time your child's No Brain behaviors elicit the particular response from you. Not all of them may apply, so just focus on the ones that do.

For example, if your child breaks a rule or throws a tantrum, you might use the "command and demand" strategy 40% of the time, use logic 20% of the time, show empathy 10% of the time, etc. What are your primary "go-to" responses when your child exhibits a No Brain behavior?

YOUR RESPONSE	PERCENTAGE
Command and demand	
Using logic/rationality	
Ignoring tantrums	
Minimizing ("it's no big deal")	
Reflecting the situation back ("I hear you saying that you're angry because…")	
Comparing their reaction to a sibling's/friend's	
Anger/Frustration/Yelling	
Empathizing ("that sounds really hard for you")	
Isolation ("go to your room," "time out," parent leaving)	
Reacting with whatever consequence or threat comes to mind	

Some of you may find it easier to take in a visual representation of how you respond to your child's No Brain behavior. If so, take your percentages from the response chart and fill in the blank pie chart that follows. We provided an example of one to give you an idea of what it might look like.

How I Respond to No Brain Behavior

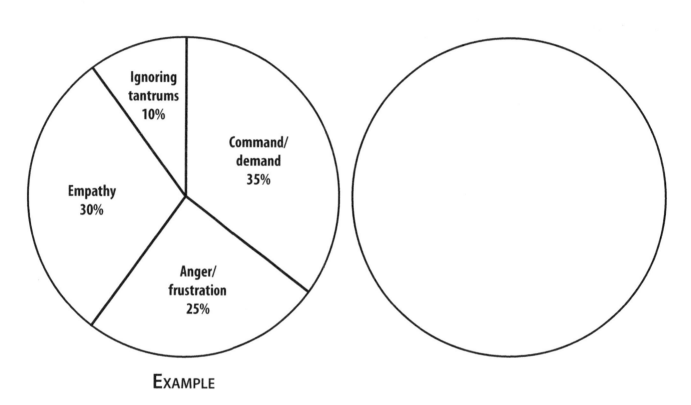

Example

Don't be hard on yourself if you're not happy with what you notice in your chart. In highly charged moments it can be hard to respond the way we'd like. Parents get triggered, too! And, we want to give you hope that with practice, responding in the ways you'd like to parent will become more automatic and easier over time. Remember, too, that there is no such thing as "perfect parenting." *Repairing* ruptures in connection is not only something that we can do, but it is important in helping our children learn that even when things are difficult, reconnection is possible. Reconnecting builds resilience.

Becoming more aware of your behavior, and how it impacts your children, is an important step toward making positive changes. When you look at your percentages in the previous chart, how often are you responding in a way that *helps* your child and calms the situation down? How often are your reactions intensifying your child's dysregulation? If you see some room for improvement, think about what you might do to shift the dynamics that aren't working for you. In other words, could you use more time alone with each child? Do you need more support from other people during certain times of the day? Do you need practice with listening but not offering solutions? Make some notes here to serve as a reminder for what you'd like to do:

_____

_____

_____

_____

_____

_____

It's important to remember that all behavior is communication, and our kids are telling us what they need in the moment, or what skills they need to learn, by the way they behave. Much of the time, kids misbehave because they *can't* control their emotions and bodies right then, not because they *won't*. Because they are not emotionally regulated or balanced in that moment, their emotions overwhelm them and become the driver of the behavior.

When you think about your children, to what extent do you think the idea that "behavior is communication" applies to them? Or do you more often think their behavior is willful or disobedient, and that they're misbehaving "on purpose" or "giving you a hard time"? Take a minute to journal briefly about one or two typical behavior patterns your child has and what they could possibly be trying to communicate—for example, *I need help tolerating transitions, I haven't learned how to express anger in ways that aren't aggressive, I don't have the executive function skills yet to plan ahead very well, I don't know how to calm myself down when I get anxious, not getting my way feels very overwhelming to me, etc.*

_____

_____

_____

_____

_____

_____

Often, seemingly out-of-control behavior is a result of underdeveloped regulation skills. However, as you'll recall from our book *The Yes Brain*, a lack of balance and frequent reactivity from your child can stem from all kinds of sources:

- Developmental age
- Temperament
- Trauma (anything that was overwhelmingly frightening or intrusive to safety)
- Sleep problems including not enough sleep
- Sensory processing challenges
- Health and medical issues
- Learning, cognitive, and other disabilities and discrepancies
- Caregivers who amplify distress or who are unresponsive
- Mismatch of environmental demands and child's capacity
- Mental health disorders

The point here isn't to make excuses for your child's unwanted behavior, but rather to put yourself in their shoes and have some empathy for their struggles. Doing this allows us to respond in a much more patient and loving way, and to teach skills, as opposed to perpetuating a cycle of No Brain reactivity.

IN THE ZONE

Children with a balanced brain are able to pause and think how best to respond to a situation, as opposed to having rigid, almost involuntary reactions to circumstances. The more opportunities we give them to practice response flexibility, the more skilled at it they become. And, the more skill they develop, the wider their window of tolerance becomes.

You'll remember from *The Yes Brain* that when your child's nervous system is balanced, they handle themselves well. We call this state "the green zone," and when they're in it, they're in a Yes Brain state. Their body, emotions, and behavior are regulated, and even when facing adversity, they feel in control and handle themselves well.

At times, negative emotions such as fear, anger, sadness, frustration, or anxiety become too intense and gain hold. All of a sudden, your child can't handle the demands of the situation and it becomes too difficult to remain calm and in the green zone.

Depending on the child and the situation, they might enter the red zone, a chaotic, explosive No Brain state categorized by aggressive or expressive behaviors such as these:

- Yelling
- Biting
- Physical or verbal aggression
- Laughing inappropriately
- Crying

Or, they may become rigid and unresponsive, entering "the blue zone," which can include taking refuge in No Brain behaviors such as:

- Shutting down
- Emotionally withdrawing
- Physically removing themselves from a situation
- Avoiding eye contact
- Dissociation

The image that follows is in black and white, but you get the idea.

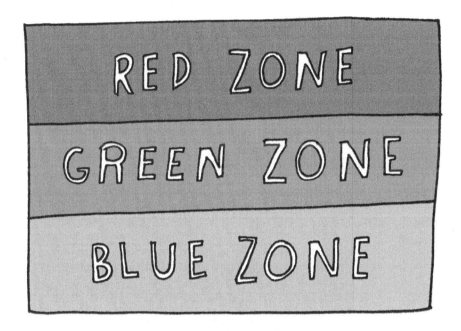

Although it's natural for kids to lose their emotional balance at times, it's important for parents to think about what triggers this sort of reactivity, how to best help them return to a state of balance, and how to expand their green zone over time. The next chapter will discuss how to expand and build your child's green zone, but here, let's focus on what you can do to help your kids get back into and remain in their green zone.

HOW BALANCED IS YOUR CHILD?

Let's start with journaling some answers to questions we posed in *The Yes Brain*. Find a comfortable place where you can write, uninterrupted, for 5 or 10 minutes. Take the time to clear your mind and focus on your individual children as you answer these questions. (Use extra sheets of paper if you're doing this for multiple children.)

What is your typical response when your kids are upset? How often is your reaction a No Brain response that threatens to move them further into the red or blue zone, as opposed to helping them return to green?

_____

_____

_____

_____

_____

How wide is my child's green zone for particular emotions? How easily do they handle discomfort, fear, anger, and disappointment?

_____

_____

_____

_____

_____

When my child becomes dysregulated, do they tend to fly into the red zone or the blue zone? How would you describe their behavior during these times?

_____

_____

_____

_____

_____

How easily does my child leave the green zone? What kind of emotion or situation does it take to send them into chaotic red or rigid blue? Are there typical triggers that lead my child toward imbalance (i.e., being hungry or tired)?

_____

_____

_____

_____

_____

What kind of social/emotional skills do they need to develop to handle the emotions and situations you described previously that may be hard for your child to handle?

_____

_____

_____

_____

How far outside the green zone does my child go? How intense is the reaction?

_____

_____

_____

_____

_____

How long does my child stay outside the green zone, and how easily does he return?

_____

_____

_____

_____

_____

What usually helps my child return to the green zone?

_____

_____

_____

_____

_____

It's understandable that at times our kids' seemingly exaggerated reactions to events can be frustrating. However, keep in mind that a No Brain response from you only sends them deeper into their own No Brain behavior. When we're reactive (and especially if we lose balance and become out of control), our children become even more reactive. By understanding their unique skills and temperament, you can respond to them in ways that not only help them achieve balance in the short term, but also teach them lifelong skills that will ultimately help them grow into teenagers and adults who can successfully navigate a complex world while staying calm and focused. As they practice being balanced, it becomes easier for them to stay balanced and return to balance more quickly.

INTEGRATION IN THE PARENT-CHILD RELATIONSHIP

Earlier, we talked about brain integration and how a Yes Brain occurs when different parts of the brain do their respective jobs, while *also* teaming up to accomplish tasks in a more effective way than they could on their own. This same concept applies to the parent-child relationship.

Integration works when people feel closely connected, but where their differences are also respected. This connection, or *linking,* comes from being able to deeply attune to your children—where you tune in to their internal state, not just their outward behavior—thus being able to help them as you notice them moving toward the red or blue zones.

In addition to linkage, which involves empathy and connection, a healthy Yes Brain parental response leaves room for *differentiation* as well. Being able to separate yourself means remembering that your job as a parent isn't to take on your children's overwhelming emotions yourself, nor is it to completely rescue them or prevent them from dealing with anything difficult. When struggles hit, you stay linked and attuned, but differentiated as well. Instead of falling apart alongside your kids, you're able to hold space for them to feel their feelings and guide them through, so they aren't left to struggle on their own.

In other words, the differentiation in the relationship means that you allow your children to experience the inevitable difficult emotions of life, but the linkage means that you stay connected enough to keep them safe and help them regain balance. This is the ultimate balance we're all striving for as parents: the Yes Brain sweet spot.

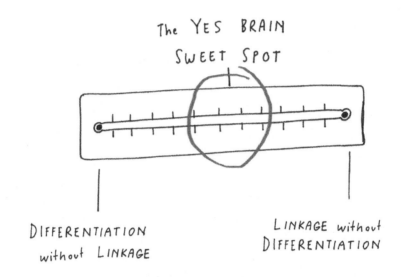

Finding the sweet spot can be hard. None of us provide optimal parenting 100% of the time. Sometimes we might be too differentiated, leading to emotionally dismissive parenting.

Emotionally dismissive parenting leads to:

Minimizing

Criticizing/Shaming

Distancing

On the other hand, sometimes there's so much linkage that we're not allowing for enough space in the relationship.

Either extreme can cause problems, both for parents and their kids. It can therefore be helpful to understand where on the spectrum your parenting style typically falls. If you look at the following graph, where would you place yourself? Are you usually more linked or more differentiated? How far in either direction would you place yourself?

Sweet Spot

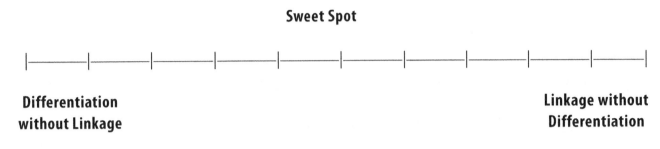

**Differentiation
without Linkage**

**Linkage without
Differentiation**

Keep this concept in mind as we move ahead.

LINKED OR ENMESHED?

Enmeshment occurs when parents are too closely linked to their children, when they feel discomfort when their kids express a range of emotions or a need for individuality. Enmeshed parents can have a narrow window of tolerance for their child's unhappiness or struggle, so they may repeatedly act on their behalf and rescue them, rather than letting them feel, try, make mistakes, and learn. Often, they have a tendency to want to bubble wrap their child, protecting them from any possible challenges.

Enmeshed parents can struggle to honor that their child is a unique separate person with different wishes, needs, emotions, and minds.

If you placed yourself closer to the Linked without Differentiation end of the scale, what do you see as the pros and cons of this style when it comes to your individual kids? Of course it's good to be connected, but are there times when you're too close to situations? Do your own childhood memories make it hard to separate how *you* feel from how your *child* feels? Is it difficult for you to let your child struggle? Does it feel as though your child's setbacks reflect on you, personally? Do you feel as though your child feels comfortable sharing his emotions and worries with you? Does he look to you for advice, or does he expect you to solve his problems for him?

Take a few minutes to think about these questions and how they relate to your relationship with your kids. What about how linked you are with your kids is working well and why? Write out your thoughts and answers here:

_____

_____

_____

_____

_____

What, if anything, feels like it's veering too much toward enmeshment? What support do you need in order to become more differentiated and move yourself closer toward the sweet spot?

_____

_____

_____

_____

_____

DIFFERENTIATED OR DISTANT?

On the other end of the integration spectrum are parents who are so differentiated that they end up becoming distant from their kids. If you think your parenting style leans more toward differentiation, what do you see as the pros and cons of parenting this way? How comfortable are you when your child shows a range of emotions? Do you feel you understand her emotional needs or motivations? Is she able to advocate for herself? Would you characterize her as being independent? Does she seem able to easily share her feelings with you? Do you two express physical or verbal affection easily? Does she ask for your advice and express her concerns with you?

As you read through these questions and think about how differentiated from your individual children you are, what about your parenting style is working and helps them find balance?

_____

_____

_____

_____

What, if anything, makes you think you might be too distant from your kids? What could you do, and what support do you need, to become more linked and move toward the sweet spot?

_____

_____

_____

_____

It's pretty clear that parenting from either end of this spectrum isn't ideal. Although changing ingrained behavior patterns may feel difficult at first, the long-term result of these shifts is a state of balance where both parent and child have what they need.

BALANCED SCHEDULE, BALANCED BRAIN

Another way to think about balance besides emotional regulation is a balanced life. One common struggle parents have these days is how to find a balance between offering their children opportunities to discover their talents and passions, and how to give them downtime where everything isn't overscheduled and overplanned. While we all want the best for our kids, it can be easy to forget that a schedule where kids have a chance to practice their emotional regulation skills through various ways of spending their time, like with friendships, spontaneous play, and free time, is crucial to the ability to achieve the goals they set.

Before we get into the details, think right now about your own schedule. In the following list, circle the phrase that most accurately describes your family's schedule:

- Way too slow
- Could use more activities
- Fairly healthy

- Maybe too busy
- Frantic

Avoid the extremes of the Integration Spectrum

Not enough linkage

Not enough differentiation

As society and priorities change, the nature of play and its perceived importance has changed as well. Free, unstructured time to play and explore has been pushed aside by replacements such as lessons, practices, activities, electronics, and media. In *The Yes Brain* we discuss the many ways that science has documented the importance of play and how essential it is for every level of our kids' development.

When you think about how your kids' days are structured, do you feel that they get enough time outside of their structured activities to play and figure out what they want to do? What percentage of their time is "downtime" where they get to actually decide how to spend their time, possibly even dealing with the boredom that can be so healthy for kids to have to face? Let's take a look at a typical week in your family.

You'll be using two different colored pens or pencils for this activity. The first color you'll use to shade in planned activities (school, piano lessons, art class, homework, baseball practice, etc.). With the second pencil you'll shade in blocks of time where your kids have nothing scheduled, where they have downtime they could use for seeing friends, tinkering, building, reading or writing for pleasure, drawing, or playing outside. We provided a couple of sample days to give you an idea of what it might look like. After reviewing it, use the blank charts that follow to fill in your children's schedules.

Key: Activity ☐ **Free** ▨ **Sleep** ☐

SAMPLE DAYS

DAY	TIME	ACTIVITY	TIME	ACTIVITY	TIME	ACTIVITY
Saturday	6 a.m.		12 p.m.	Free time	6 p.m.	Dinner
	7 a.m.		1 p.m.	Lunch	7 p.m.	Free time
	8 a.m.	Breakfast	2 p.m.	Drive	8 p.m.	Free time
	9 a.m.	Soccer practice	3 p.m.	Doctor appointment	9 p.m.	
	10 a.m.	Soccer practice	4 p.m.	Free time	10 p.m.	
	11 a.m.	Free time	5 p.m.	Practice piano	11 p.m.	

DAY	TIME	ACTIVITY	TIME	ACTIVITY	TIME	ACTIVITY
Wednesday	7:00 a.m.	Breakfast	2:30 p.m.	School ends	7:00 p.m.	Free time
	8:00 a.m.	School	3:00 p.m.	Art class	8:30 p.m.	Bedtime
		School	4:00 p.m.	Art class		
		School	4:30 p.m.	Homework		
		School	5:30 p.m.	Homework		
		School	6:00 p.m.	Dinner		
		School	6:30 p.m.	Free time		

DAY	TIME	ACTIVITY	TIME	ACTIVITY	TIME	ACTIVITY

DAY	TIME	ACTIVITY	TIME	ACTIVITY	TIME	ACTIVITY

DAY	TIME	ACTIVITY	TIME	ACTIVITY	TIME	ACTIVITY

DAY	TIME	ACTIVITY	TIME	ACTIVITY	TIME	ACTIVITY

DAY	TIME	ACTIVITY	TIME	ACTIVITY	TIME	ACTIVITY

DAY	TIME	ACTIVITY	TIME	ACTIVITY	TIME	ACTIVITY

DAY	TIME	ACTIVITY	TIME	ACTIVITY	TIME	ACTIVITY

The point of the exercise is to get a visual sense of what your child's schedule looks like. Is it overscheduled? Is there enough downtime? Are there places where you could make changes to have the day feel more balanced? When you think about your child's moods and behavior, does it feel as though your child could use more free time spread throughout the day as opposed to having it all at the end of the day? Is your child getting enough sleep?

As you think about the charts you've made, write some notes here about what you think might be working well, and what, if anything, you'd like to change:

_____

_____

_____

_____

_____

_____

We're not saying that a busy schedule is inherently bad. Just that free time is key. Play is where children develop so many of the skills they need to be successful later in life.

Some kids actually thrive on having more activities, while some suffer from it. Here are some questions to help you consider whether your own child is overscheduled.

1. Does my child seem frequently tired or grumpy, or demonstrate other indicators of imbalance, such as showing signs of being under pressure or feeling anxious? Is my kid stressed out?

2. Is my child so busy that they don't have unstructured time for playing and being creative?

3. Is my child getting enough sleep? (If your child is involved in so many activities that they're just getting started on homework at bedtime, that's a problem).

4. Is my child's schedule so full that they don't have time to hang out with friends or siblings?

5. Are we all too busy to eat dinner together regularly? (You don't have to eat every meal together, but if you're rarely eating together, that's a concern).

6. Are you saying "hurry up" all the time to your children?

7. Are you so active and stressed that a majority of your interactions are reactive and impatient?

Take a few minutes with these questions. Do you feel any concern about the pace of your current family calendar? Anything you think ought to change?

WHAT YOU CAN DO: YES BRAIN STRATEGIES THAT PROMOTE BALANCE

At the end of each of the main chapters of this workbook, we'll discuss specific strategies to help promote the particular Yes Brain fundamental we're discussing.

Yes Brain Strategy #1 for Promoting a Balanced Brain — Maximize the ZZZs

We hear all the time that sleep is important. How much do you prioritize getting your child enough sleep? Here's what the American Academy of Sleep Medicine, whose guidelines have been endorsed by the American Academy of Pediatrics, recommends for each respective age group:

HOW MUCH SLEEP DO KIDS NEED?

AGES	⇒	HOURS
4-12 months	⇒	12-16 (including naps)
1-2 years	⇒	11-14 (including naps)
3-5 years	⇒	10-13 (including naps)
6-12 years	⇒	9-12
13-18 years	⇒	8-10

* These are just recommendations.
Every child is different, and each person's need for sleep varies.

How are you doing at hitting these marks in your family? Do you feel as though your family is getting the amount of sleep they need? Who is and who isn't? Any specific reasons why? Fill in your answers here:

_____

_____

_____

_____

In *The Yes Brain*, we highlight several factors that can get in the way of kids getting enough sleep. As you read through them, think about how each factor affects sleep in your home, and what specific steps you can take to address the problem. If any of them resonate with you, then fill in the blanks as they apply to you.

A schedule that's too full.

• Are there so many activities that bedtime is being pushed later and later?

Today our schedule feels very _____.
                                (adjective)

_____ has _____ activities. We'll arrive home at _____.
  (person in family)   (number)   (time)

This means bedtime will be at _____.
                                  (time)

I'd prefer if bedtime was at _____.
                                  (time)

In order to make that happen, I will _____

_____.

I might also need to _____

_____.

Making these changes could result in my child getting more sleep, and that could lead to:

_____

_____

A chaotic or noisy environment.

- Is the neighborhood or home too noisy or bright?
- Are there other people (including siblings) in the home that make it hard for your child to sleep?

The environment in and around our home is _____.
(adjective)

My child's bedroom environment is _____.
(adjective)

My child finds it easiest to fall asleep when his or her environment is

_____. I can create this environment for them by
        (adjective)

_____

and _____.

If this feels difficult to do myself, I can ask _____ for help.
(person)

Making these changes could result in my child getting more sleep, and that could lead to:

_____

_____

Parental work hours.

- Is waiting for a parent to get home causing meals or bedtime to start too late?

_____ arrives home at _____.
        (person)   (time)

We usually wait for _____ to _____.
                    (same person)   (activity)

This means bedtime is at _____. I'd like bedtime to be at _____.
                        (time)   (time)

In order to make that happen, I will _____.

I might also need to _____.

To make sure _____ still has time with our child, we can
                    (same person)

_____.

If I need help, I can _____ or _____.
                              (verb)   (verb)

Making these changes could result in my child getting more sleep, and that could lead to:

_____

_____

Bedtime struggles.
- Is there a negative connotation associated with bedtime that results in resistance?
- Is the bedtime routine rushed?

Putting my child to sleep is _____.
                                    (adjective)

We start the bedtime routine at _____.
                                      (time)

I return to the room after saying goodnight _____ times, on average.
                                                 (number)

It generally takes _____ minutes to put my child to sleep.
                        (number)

My child sees bedtime as _____ and _____.
                                (adjective)   (adjective)

My mood before bedtime can best be described as _____.
                                                        (adjective)

I often feel _____ and _____ during our bedtime routine.
                  (adjective)   (adjective)

I'd like to change this so our bedtime routine can be more _____

(adjective)

and _____.

(adjective)

To help my child think more positively about bedtime I can _____

and _____.

To help make my attitude more positive, I can _____

and _____.

Making these changes could result in my child getting more sleep, and that could lead to:

_____

_____

Not enough time to "ramp down."

• Is there enough time for children to wind down and relax before they're expected to sleep?

My child's bedtime is at _____. We turn off electronics at _____.

(time)   (time)

One hour before bed my child is _____ and their mood can be

(activity)

best described as _____.

(adjective)

Thirty minutes before bed my child is _____ and their mood

(activity)

can be best described as _____.

(adjective)

I would like my child to be more _____ and _____

(adjective)   (adjective) at bedtime and to make that happen I will _____ and

(verb)

_____ .

(verb)

If I need extra support making these changes I can _____

(verb)

or _____ .

(verb)

Making these changes could result in my child getting more sleep, and that could lead to:

_____

_____

As you can see, there are many different factors that can affect a child's ability to get a good night's sleep. Some of the changes may be simple for you to make; others may take a bit more effort or may need to be shifted multiple times before you get them right. But once you see the improvement in your child's moods, behaviors, and ability to stay in their Yes Brain, you may wish you had started sooner!

Yes Brain Strategy #2 for Promoting a Balanced Brain — Serve a Healthy Mind Platter

Just like you want to serve your kids a balanced diet of food, it's important that they develop a life that provides them with a healthy mental and emotional balance as well. This is what we call a Healthy Mind Platter. Here's what it looks like:

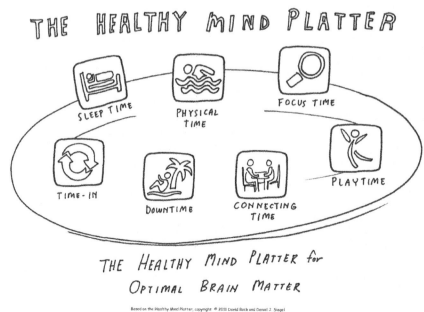

THE HEALTHY MIND PLATTER

SLEEP TIME

PHYSICAL TIME

FOCUS TIME

TIME-IN

DOWNTIME

CONNECTING TIME

PLAYTIME

THE HEALTHY MIND PLATTER for OPTIMAL BRAIN MATTER

As you can see from this illustration, there are seven daily essential mental activities that optimize brain matter and create balance and well-being.

- **Focus time:** When we closely focus on tasks in a goal-oriented way, we take on challenges that make deep connections in the brain.
- **Playtime:** When we allow ourselves to be spontaneous or creative, playfully enjoying novel experiences, we make new connections in the brain.
- **Connecting time:** When we connect with other people, ideally in person, and when we take time to appreciate our connection to the natural world around us, we activate and reinforce the brain's relational circuitry.
- **Physical time:** When we move our body, aerobically if medically possible, we strengthen the brain in many ways.
- **Time-in:** When we quietly reflect internally, focusing on sensations, images, feelings, and thoughts, we help to better integrate the brain.
- **Downtime:** When we are unfocused, without any specific goal, and let our mind wander or simply relax, we help the brain recharge.
- **Sleep time:** When we give the brain the rest it needs, we consolidate learning and recover from the experiences of the day.

Depending on your child, and your family, some of these activities will come more naturally than others. Which of them do you feel you're best at making sure your kids have?

_____

_____

_____

Which do you feel you need to work on making sure your kids get more of?

_____

_____

_____

Now that you've gotten clear about which of the seven activities are harder for you to keep in your kids' routine, think about what *keeps* you from getting your kids what they need?

Do you think you or your child's temperament affects your ability to access all seven activities? For example, do you tend to enjoy time-in or connecting time more than physical time?

Is it easier to get your child to agree to creative time than focus time? If temperament is part of what holds you back, what would you need to change in order to bring about more balance?

_____

_____

_____

So many of us feel we have to fill our children's time with "enrichment" and opportunities to ensure future success, but there are only so many hours in a day. To what extent do you feel pressured to, for example, shortchange physical time or downtime because concentrating more on focus time may result in better grades or more external accomplishments?

_____

_____

_____

How hard is it for you to take a step away from the treadmill of success? Do you feel like you're gambling with your child's future?

_____

_____

_____

What sort of support would you need to bring more balance to your child's Healthy Mind Platter? Who would you need help from? What would you have to do?

_____

_____

_____

When we allow our children to have access to a wide variety of mental activities, we give them the opportunity to develop in different ways, and to wire their brains to recognize and feel the effects of a healthy and balanced life.

YES BRAIN KIDS: TEACH YOUR KIDS ABOUT BALANCE

One of the best ways you can help your kids live their lives with more balance is to teach them to think about the concept themselves. With that in mind, we've created these illustrations that you can read with your child. These are written with five- to nine-year-olds in mind, but feel free to adapt them to the age of your children.

Yes Brain Kids: Teach Your Kids About Balance

You know how you feel when it just seems like everything is going right and you handle yourself well? We call this being in the green zone.

But sometimes you get upset. You might get really mad, or maybe scared or nervous. You might want to cry or yell. This is what we call being in the red zone.

Or maybe when you get upset you pull away from everyone, wanting to be quiet, and by yourself. Maybe your body feels limp, like a noodle. This is called going into the blue zone.

Here's a simple strategy you can use whenever you're upset and want to move back into the green. Just put one hand on your chest, and one hand on your stomach. Try that now, and just sit there breathing, with a hand on your chest, and a hand on your stomach. See how calm you feel?

Now, tonight, when you're getting sleepy and your eyelids are getting heavy and your body is starting to feel relaxed, practice this trick again. Then each night, just before bed, practice it again, and notice how calm it makes you feel.

Yes Brain Kids: Teach Your Kids About Balance

Olivia used this strategy when her friends at school didn't invite her to play with them. It hurt to be left out, and she felt herself entering the blue zone. She started to cry, and just wanted to disappear.

But she noticed the blue-zone feelings and calmed herself by putting her hands over her heart and stomach. She felt better right away and moved back into the green zone. She still felt a little sad, but she knew she'd be okay.

The next time something makes you feel sad, or angry, or afraid, use this tool. With practice, you'll get to where you can use it at any time to help you move back into the green zone when you need to.

For most children, understanding this concept begins with teaching them to recognize the feeling of being out of balance. This often starts with simply encouraging them to talk about how they feel, giving words to their feelings that extend beyond "good" and "bad," and then helping guide them back to a state of equilibrium through methods like deep breathing, physical connection, and mindfulness. Once back in a state of balance, help them talk about the difference they feel when they're in the green zone versus the red or blue zones. The ability to verbalize your emotions is a quick way to reduce their effect on you and return to the green zone.

One way to help your child find balance is through mindful self-compassion. A very simple way of helping your child understand this method is to explain that self-compassion involves treating yourself as you would a friend. Mindfulness involves being aware of your feelings in the moment, self-compassion means asking what you need in that moment.

For example, if making mistakes is something that tends to throw your child into the red or blue zone, encourage them to imagine, instead, that it's a friend who has that thought about themselves. How would you speak to the friend to help them feel better?

If your friend made a mistake, would you say to them, "Well, you made that mistake because you're stupid. You never do the right thing. You're never going to understand how to do this right because you're just a loser"? No, of course not. But often that's how we talk to ourselves. To a friend you might say something more like, "Everyone makes mistakes sometimes. It's OK. Nothing bad happened. Mistakes are how we learn how to get better at things!"

With this in mind, have your child write a letter to themselves (or help them write it), as if they were talking to a friend. Ask them to imagine their friend is struggling with the same feelings that throw your child out of the green zone.

What would you say to help them feel better?

_____

_____

_____

_____

How would you encourage them?

_____

_____

_____

_____

What can you say to help calm them down and return to the green zone?

_____

_____

_____

_____

Research shows that the way we talk to ourselves has long-term effects on how we view ourselves. This letter writing can eventually transition to compassionate self-talk. Encourage your child to speak to themselves as they would to a friend: kindly. In the moment of upset, this sort of understanding self-talk will help return their emotions to a state of calm and, over time, bring about more resilience when faced with challenges.

MY OWN YES BRAIN: PROMOTING BALANCE IN MYSELF

Each of the main chapters of *The Yes Brain* concludes by helping parents think about how they can apply the concepts of the chapter to their own lives. Here, we want to help you think about how balanced you feel in your own life.

As adults, most of us live with a certain amount of stress and pressure every day. We get pulled in multiple directions at any given time. Whether it's our children, our career, our extended family, our community, or something else, it can be a struggle to maintain balance. And so many parents put their own well-being at the bottom of the list.

How balanced are your days, and how healthy is your mind platter? How easily do you incorporate the seven essential activities into your own life? Which ones are easiest for you? Which are the most difficult?

Think back to the questions you answered earlier about what keeps you from integrating certain aspects of the Healthy Mind Platter into your kids' days. How much of this reasoning keeps you from doing the same for yourself? What would you need to be able to bring all seven activities into your day? Take a few minutes and write your thoughts here:

_____

_____

_____

_____

_____

Next, we've split the pie chart that follows into 24 one-hour segments. Think about a typical day and fill in where you would generally spend your focus time, downtime, playtime, and so on. It's important to remember that no parent is perfect, so this isn't meant to put pressure on you to be perfectly balanced all the time (or to make your kids be). But aiming for balance will help create a Yes Brain mindset for yourself, which of course will help you do so for your kids.

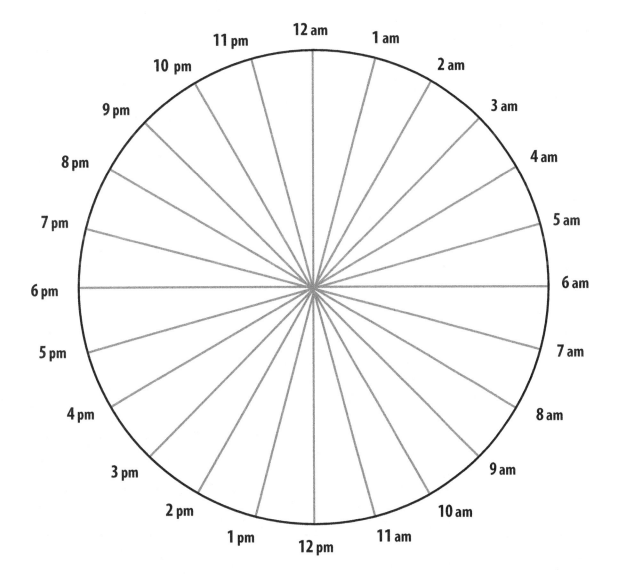

When you step back and look at your chart, does it look balanced to you? Do you see anywhere you might be able to make some shifts in order to incorporate an activity that might be missing, or where you're spending too much time on one activity, but not enough in another? Give some thought to this and create another version of your day in this second blank chart.

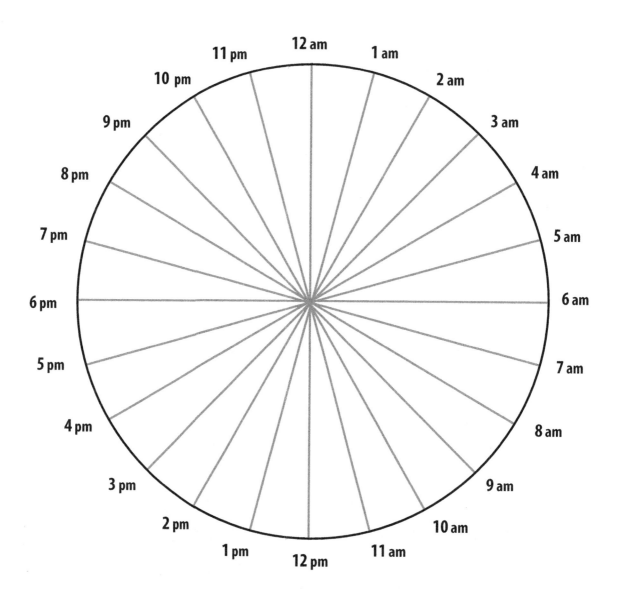

Keep working on it until you feel it's closer to being balanced and still feels like something you can keep up with. You may need to start small and just add in 20 minutes of time-in or 20 minutes of physical time or shave off just 30 minutes of focus time. Remember, it's not perfection you're striving for. It's balance. It's about cultivating and creating more wellness for ourselves.

Once you've got a plan you feel you can stick with, follow it for a few days and journal each day about what you notice. Does your body feel different? If so, how? Are your interactions with your family different in any way? What do you notice? Does your wheel still need adjusting? What would you like to change? How can you make that happen?

Keep journaling as your week passes. Note positive changes so you continue to reinforce the behavior. Note any difficulties as well so you can be aware of what shifts you may still want to make. You can start your journaling here, but you may want to get yourself a small notebook or a pad of paper so you can continue past the first day.

Finding balance is a process. But even small steps will have you noticing big changes. Keep it up!

CHAPTER 3

Resilience

The wider a child's window of tolerance for difficult times and uncomfortable emotions, the more resilient they can be in the face of adversity, instead of falling apart when things don't go their way. Resilience is also about bouncing back, about how readily they are able to move from the red or blue zone back into the green zone—how they can return from chaos or rigidity and get back into the harmony within the window.

—The Yes Brain

The second Yes Brain fundamental is resilience. You'll remember from the previous chapter that we discussed helping kids become more balanced so they can do a better job of staying in the green zone when things don't go their way. In this chapter we'll take a look at encouraging resilience and grit in our kids, which is about not only staying in the green zone, but also *expanding and strengthening* it. Widening our children's window of tolerance for difficult times and uncomfortable emotions helps them to be more resilient in the face of adversity.

In a No Brain state, kids are unable to control their own bodies, emotions, and decisions. Caught in this cycle, their worries and anxieties keep them feeling as though everything is too much for them to handle. We want, instead, for them to develop Yes Brain resilience and know that they have the skills—or can learn the skills—needed to overcome any adversities they may face in life.

THE GOAL: SKILL-BUILDING INSTEAD OF EXTINGUISHING UNWANTED BEHAVIOR

Picture, for a moment, that your child is behaving in a way you don't like. Maybe they're fighting with their sibling, or refusing to take a bath before bedtime, or arguing with you about how much screen time they should be allowed.

What emotions come up for you when your child behaves like this *(anger, frustration, embarrassment, etc.)?* Write your thoughts here:

_____

_____

_____

_____

How do you think about your child in these moments when they misbehave? *("He's always rude." "Why is she so obnoxious when she doesn't get what she wants?" "They're ridiculous; why won't they just clean up their room when I ask?" "She's just spoiled.").* While we know that you don't think about your kids this way all the time, being frustrated with them is normal. For some people, it can lead to thinking this way when, once again, you're faced with a child who's not doing what you want. Be as honest with yourself as possible and write your internal monologue here:

_____

_____

_____

_____

What is your main goal when your kids act in a way you don't like? (i.e., *stop the behavior as quickly as possible, remind my kids of the rules, show people that I'm a good parent, control them, teach them, etc.).* Write your goals here:

_____

_____

_____

_____

For so many of us, our unconscious and immediate reaction when our children are behaving in a way we don't like is to attempt to extinguish that behavior or make them "knock it off!" While that end goal is totally understandable, it's important to remember that all behavior is communication. Problematic behavior is our child's way of telling us they need help building certain skills. The goal, then, instead of focusing on stopping the behavior, is to build the skills your child hasn't mastered yet so that they have effective tools to handle the situation better next time, or over time as development unfolds.

Instead of trying to extinguish bad behavior ...

Build skills that lead to resilience and wellbeing

Instead of focusing on extinguishing the problem ...

View behavior as communication and focus on building skills

The saying, "Your child isn't giving you a hard time, they're *having* a hard time" is very apt in this instance. The key for us, as parents, is to be able to shift our perspective so we respond to their behavior with this in mind—in other words, responding to the child's needs, as opposed to reacting to the child's behaviors. One of the best ways to do this is to reframe the language we use when we talk about their behavior.

Earlier in this chapter we asked you to write down how you think about your kids when they're behaving in a way you don't like. If your thoughts sometimes run along the lines of, "*He's just doing this for attention*" or "*She's so bossy,*" let's see how you can reframe those moments.

In the left column, write down the thoughts you have when your child is behaving in ways you don't like. These may be internal thoughts, or even how you talk about the incidents with other people. In the middle column, you're going to reframe the sentence so you're approaching the situation with a more curious mind. And finally, in the right column, make some notes about how you can help build the skills your child might need to learn based on their behavior. We provided you with two examples and space to add in your own.

INTERNAL MONOLOGUE	REFRAME	SKILLS
She's always so bossy! It's so frustrating when she demands things from me.	*Wow. She's really having a hard time being patient. I wonder what she needs in order to learn how to wait without getting upset.*	*Patience. Maybe doing some activities together that require being patient in order to get what we want—maybe baking. Positive reinforcement when she's able to wait. Start small! Five minutes to a child can feel like hours!*
He has a rage problem. He's going to get himself in a lot of trouble.	*He has a hard time with self-control when he gets angry. He needs some practice expressing big feelings without hurting someone else, and communicating his anger in more appropriate ways.*	*Expressing feelings in helpful ways. We can talk about what it feels like to be really angry and brainstorm what he can do instead of hitting, and practice running or jumping or doing something else when he's mad.*

By being curious about what might be causing your child's behavior, you allow yourself to respond to them with a mindset that's geared toward helping them learn a missing skill, as opposed to simply wanting the behavior to go away. As you continue this approach, over time, those behaviors become less frequent because they're no longer needed. And your child continues to develop their Yes Brain along with building those resiliency skills!

RESILIENCE, RECEPTIVITY, AND EXPANDING THE GREEN ZONE

To a large extent, when we talk about resilience, we're talking about helping kids be *receptive* to what life hands them, as opposed to being *reactive* about it. Kids who are reactive are kids who struggle with the world around them not going as planned. They're always at the mercy of their surroundings—be it other people, events, changes in plans, etc. Receptivity, however, allows your child to observe and assess their surroundings, then *choose* how to respond.

REACTIVITY blocks RESILIENCE

RECEPTIVITY promotes it

That's why we started with the idea of balance. If a child is balanced and in control of their emotions, they can remain more receptive. They can stay in the green zone more often. Kids in the green zone still feel big feelings, but they have a much easier time staying balanced in the midst of those big feelings, and accessing their upstairs brain (making good decisions, listening, understanding, considering consequences, and so on).

Thus, the long-term goal is to expand that green zone so that receptivity and resilience become the default response.

SHORT-TERM GOAL: BALANCE
(getting back into the green zone)

LONG-TERM GOAL: RESILIENCE
(expanding the green zone)

As they continue to learn how to get back into the green zone, your child's window of tolerance widens. And as it widens, they're more capable of handling setbacks or challenging emotions and situations.

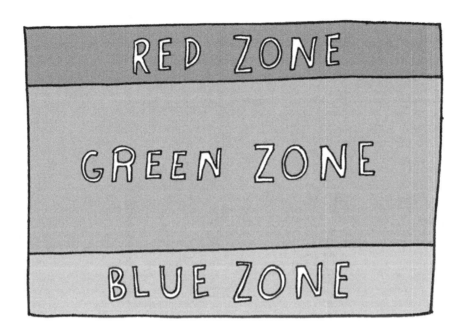

We asked before how easy it is for your child to return to the green zone once he's left it. That's more about regaining balance. Now, in this activity, we want you to think more about how wide your child's green zone actually is. How easily does he lose control when things get hard? Living life with a narrow green zone is tough for anyone, so understanding how wide your child's is, lets you better help her.

What sends your child out of the green zone? It might be internal triggers like stress, anxiety, pain, or feeling out of control. For some, external triggers like feeling judged, being alone too much, loud noises, or crowded spaces are what's hard to handle. Sometimes it's a combination of both. Take this time to think about what tends to send your child into the red or blue zones and write them down here:

_____

_____

_____

_____

Letting Kids Face Difficulties and Challenges

Part of what widens the window of tolerance for our kids is allowing them to face adversity, to feel negative emotions, and even to fail. While it's natural for parents to want to protect their kids from pain and disappointment, teaching kids that they have the ability to cope with and to recover from their struggles is what ultimately builds their resilient Yes Brain.

We're not suggesting you let your kids simply flounder and struggle. Rather, we're suggesting you consider how much you rescue or protect them from struggling, versus how much you show them that you're there to help and support them as they get through their frustrations and failures.

Expand the Green Zone

Because we all want the best for our kids, it can be hard to recognize when we're actually doing *too much*, denying our kids the opportunity to rise to the occasion and function well on their own. Let's take a look at how you respond when your kids are having a difficult time. Below you'll see a series of statements focused on this topic. How many of the sentences below feel as though they accurately describe the way you parent your child?

1. I can't handle it when I see my child struggle.

    o Agree

    o Disagree

2. I can't tolerate it when my child fails.

    o Agree

    o Disagree

3. I intervene frequently with other adults about how they treat my child.

    o Agree

    o Disagree

4. It's hard for me to let my child make their own choices.

    o Agree

    o Disagree

5. I get into power struggles with my child over little things.

    o Agree

    o Disagree

6. I have worries and concerns about my child that other parents don't seem to have.

    o Agree

    o Disagree

7. I sometimes wonder if I expect too much from my child.

    o Agree

    o Disagree

8. I sometimes wonder if I expect too little from my child.

    o Agree

    o Disagree

9. My child has very few responsibilities.

    o Agree

    o Disagree

10. I often help my child before they ask me to.

    o Agree

    o Disagree

All of these statements are a sign that you may be overparenting your child. How many did you agree with? _____

Did any of them surprise you?

_____

_____

Which areas do you think you can easily make some changes in?

_____

_____

_____

_____

Which areas seem more challenging for you?

_____

_____

_____

_____

Do you see ways you're getting in the way of your child learning and building skills because you're doing too much for them? Explain.

_____

_____

_____

_____

Overparenting stems from many places. Sometimes the parent is trying to manage their own discomfort with the child's suffering, some may be trying to micromanage events to control their own anxiety, still others may feel guilty about setting boundaries. It usually comes from a good place, but it ends up not serving our children well in the long run. What we're looking for isn't perfection, it's balance and resilience. Allowing your child to try and to fail and to see they can survive helps increase their window of tolerance (their green zone) for challenges. The wider their green zone is, the more resilient they become to setbacks.

Pushin' and Cushion

You'll remember the phrase "pushin' and cushion" is about knowing when to step in to help, and when to let your kids struggle through a challenging situation. Sometimes kids need practice to move beyond what's comfortable for them (pushin') and sometimes obstacles are just too big to handle on their own and they need some extra support to get through it (cushion). It's important to remember that pushin' only works if it's not too much for your child's nervous system. If they get flooded and veer off into the red or blue zones, pull back and perhaps try some cushion with baby steps toward your goal.

When you think about how your child responds to something that's challenging for them, what would you say is more often necessary: pushing them or cushioning them? Most kids need a combination, so think about what your individual child is more likely to need. It's not always easy to know, but these questions should help it become clearer.

What is your child's temperament and developmental stage, and what do they need right now? Stay attuned to your child's actual internal experience, revealed by their signals and communication, not what you think they should be feeling.

_____

_____

_____

_____

_____

Are you clear on what the real issue is? Talk to your child and get clear on what the real issue is (it may not be what you assume). Then you can help problem-solve.

_____

_____

_____

_____

Sometimes parents need to provide the pushin'...

And sometimes kids need more cushion.

What messages do you send about risk taking and failure? What explicit and implicit messages are you sending about taking risks, "being careful," divergent thinking, whether "failure" is ever acceptable, etc.?

_____

_____

_____

_____

What skills does your child need in order to handle potential (and inevitable) failure? Again, the goal isn't to protect your children from failure but to help build skills that lead to overcoming adversity.

_____

_____

_____

_____

What tools are you giving your child to help them return to and expand their green zone? For example, the ability to calm themselves down and regain control once they've moved into the red or blue zone.

_____

_____

_____

_____

Remember, every child is different, and complex. In each situation, make decisions about what's best for this unique child in this particular moment, and what will lead to growth and expansion of what they think they can do.

WHAT YOU CAN DO: YES BRAIN STRATEGIES THAT PROMOTE RESILIENCE

Yes Brain Strategy #1 for Promoting a Resilient Brain—Shower Your Kids with the Four S's

As with just about everything else when it comes to parenting, relationships are the key to building resilience. Kids are more likely to have the confidence to tackle new or uncomfortable challenges when they have a deep feeling of acceptance and support behind them. This kind of connected care allows your kids to experience the four S's:

Shower Your Kids
with the Four S's

S afe

S een

S oothed

S ecure

When the four S's are a part of a child's life in a consistent (not perfect) way, they know they have a safe base from which they can venture out, and a place to return to if things get too hard. This secure base allows kids to step out into the unknown and develop the confidence and grit to tackle whatever life sends their way. While you obviously know what these words mean, in the context of your children, we define them this way:

- **Safe:** where they feel protected and sheltered from harm.
- **Seen:** where they know you care about them, understand them, and pay attention to them.
- **Soothed:** where they know you'll be there for them and help them when they're hurting.
- **Secure:** develops from the other S's so they trust you to predictably help them feel "at home" in the world, then learn to help *themselves* feel safe, seen, and soothed. Security develops when our children come to know that even when there are ruptures in the first three S's, a repair will be reliably initiated and reconnection established.

Let's take a moment to consider how well you think you're doing with providing your kids with their daily dose of the Four S's. Start by choosing two different colored pens or pencils for this exercise. One color to represent you, and the other to represent your child. Using the following blank graph chart, on a scale of 1–5, using your color, place a mark where you'd rate yourself on making sure your kids consistently (not perfectly) feel safe, seen, soothed, and secure. Next, take the other color and, using the 1–5 scale, place a mark where you'd rate your child's *need* for that particular S (e.g., some kids just feel naturally more secure. Or you may have been doing a great job with making sure your kids feel safe, but less so when it comes to making sure they feel soothed when they need it). We provided a sample chart.

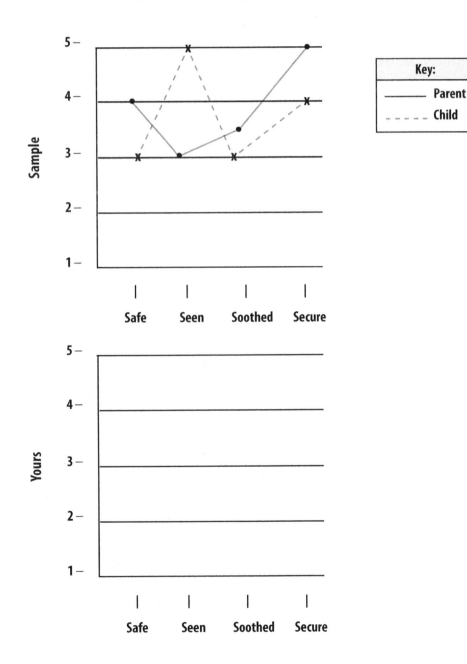

Now that you've graphed your four S's, are there any areas where you feel like you could increase (or decrease) what you're doing so you match your child's specific needs? On the lines that follow, write what specific steps you could take to achieve that (*showing interest in their interests, spending one-on-one time, repairing after a conflict, etc.*). The more specific you are about how you'll make it happen, the more likely it will be to actually happen.

_____

_____

_____

_____

By the way, if you'd like to learn more about the four S's, take a look at our recent book, *The Power of Showing Up*, where we focus on this concept throughout the entire book.

Yes Brain Strategy #2 for Promoting a Resilient Brain — Teach Mindsight Skills

Mindsight is a term Dan coined that means, in its simplest form, the ability to perceive and understand your own mind and the mind of others. By helping our kids develop Mindsight skills, we give them an opportunity to gain more control over their emotions and impulses, allow them to more fully understand their own mind and body, and improve their relationships with other people.

This is a concept we emphasize in virtually all of our writing because it's about helping kids obtain the crucial skills of insight, empathy, and integration. They help us learn to monitor and then modify our inner experience. Once this happens, kids can understand and harness the power of their minds to change the way they view and respond to their circumstances. In other words, they can expand their green zones.

Let's talk about a few different ways to help kids get control over their behaviors and actions during difficult situations.

Socratic Questioning

Explain to your child that how we feel at any given moment is driven by the thoughts and beliefs we have—sometimes ones we're not even aware of having. And the thing about thoughts is that just because we think them, it doesn't mean they're true! Socratic questioning is a way to slow down and explore the thoughts that are keeping you stuck in the red or blue zone.

Begin by asking your child for a negative thought they have when they notice they're stuck in their No Brain (*i.e., I'm no good at sports, I'm going to fail my test, my friends don't like me anymore*).

This sort of critical thinking can lead to a broadened perspective that can help widen your child's window of tolerance. They'll then be less easily thrown off by upsets and challenges and can stay in the green zone (or come back to it) more easily.

This is now "the thought to be questioned." You can write it down here:

_____

_____

_____

_____

Next, have them question this belief (feel free to adapt the language to suit your child's age):

What is the evidence for this thought? What is the evidence against it?

_____

_____

_____

_____

Am I basing this thought on facts or feelings?

_____

_____

_____

_____

Could I be misinterpreting the evidence? Am I making assumptions?

_____

_____

_____

_____

Might other people see the situation differently? How would they interpret the evidence?

_____

_____

_____

_____

Am I looking at all the evidence, or just what supports my thoughts?

_____

_____

_____

_____

Could my thoughts be an exaggeration of what's true?

_____

_____

_____

Am I having the thought out of habit? Or do the facts support it?

_____

_____

_____

_____

Did someone pass this thought on to me? If so, are they a reliable source?

_____

_____

_____

Is my thought a likely scenario, or a worst-case scenario?

_____

_____

_____

_____

Five Points of Focus

This is a simple grounding exercise that's particularly good for regaining control of racing thoughts, anxiety, and stress. This mindfulness practice brings you back to the present moment by using your five senses.

1. Look around and name five things you see. Try to do it slowly and notice each one.

2. Next, name four things you hear. Again, focus in on the sounds.

3. Now name three things you can feel *(e.g., the waistband of your pants, the chair you're sitting on, your feet in your shoes)*. Notice how each one is different from the other.

4. Then name two things you can smell. If you're not somewhere that's likely to provide too many scents, perhaps walk to the kitchen and open the refrigerator.

5. And finally, one thing you can taste *(most likely this will be the inside of your mouth, so perhaps gum, toothpaste, whatever you last ate)*. Whatever it is, focus on it for a moment.

This exercise helps bring your thoughts back into the present moment and out of being stuck on future worries or past regrets. Feeling out of control because of your mind and body's reaction to challenges can be very unsettling. Learning how to ground yourself and come back to the green zone puts control back in your child's hands.

Draw It Out

Some people learn much more easily using visual aids. You've noticed we use cartoons in our books as a way to really make our points clear. Similarly, one of the best ways we've found for helping children understand how their behavior affects others is by literally drawing the event and giving the child a chance to see what each person might have been thinking in the moment using thought bubbles.

• Don't worry if you can't draw! Stick figures are literally perfect for this exercise. As long as you can draw stick figures and a thought bubble over their heads, you're good to go.

• To begin, take a recent incident where your child's mood or behavior made a situation more difficult. Later, we provide the example of a playdate disagreement (please adapt the idea to suit your child's age). On the next page, we have a stick figure representing each person involved. And each one has a talk bubble with what they said out loud.

• You can begin simply, *"Let's talk about what happened when your friends were here earlier. I know you were pretty upset."* And then explain that you're going to draw it so it's easier to understand everything that happened.

So, you might draw the incident while you describe it to your child: "*You wanted to play pirates. Your friends didn't want to do the same games as you did. And you started to go into the red zone. Then they also went into the red zone!*"

"*I wonder what they were thinking when you insisted that they follow your idea.*"

"I wonder…" is the beginning of understanding Mindsight. Encourage your child to consider what each friend might have been thinking when this event happened. If it's easier, your child can start with himself. As you encourage insight and empathy from your child ("*Why do you think Max started to cry? I wonder why Olivia got so mad? What do you think they might have been feeling?*" And, "*What were you thinking or feeling right before you went into the red zone?*"), draw another set of stick figures—this time with thought bubbles to show each child's *inner experience* at the time. Of course you don't know for sure what each person thought, but because we have Mindsight, you might say something like, "*Do you think maybe Max felt sad because you didn't like his idea?*"

2. FRIEND A   FRIEND B   MY CHILD

Why doesn't she like my idea? Maybe she doesn't like me either.

Loud voices scare me. I feel uncomfortable.

I don't know how to ride a bike. I will be embarrassed!

As you work through and narrate what each person might have been thinking or feeling, ask your child how they might have the same conversation next time to get a better result. If it feels helpful, you can draw a second set of drawings with the alternate conversation and the alternate guesses at thoughts and feelings.

Learning to step outside of their own feelings and look at how what they're doing or saying is affecting others is a fundamental aspect of gaining insight and empathy. This is Mindsight.

YES BRAIN KIDS: TEACH YOUR KIDS ABOUT RESILIENCE

In the last chapter's "Yes Brain Kids" we introduced the concept of the green zone and what it looks like to leave it and enter the red or blue zones. This chapter focuses on resilience and talking directly to your kids about handling upsets, that it's OK to feel challenged by difficulties that life brings us, and that they also have the power to control how they feel and react to these circumstances. As we've said, sometimes those upsetting moments are times of ruptures in our connection that can be repaired. As parents, we can teach our kids the important lesson of resilience, that even when things are difficult, they can be made better. In other words, depending on how we respond, we have the opportunity to either be at the mercy of emotions and circumstances, or to learn from the struggles we face and make a repair and reconnection. Sometimes leaving the green zone is from our own emotional storms, creating a kind of disconnection internally that can also be seen as something in need of soothing and reconnection.

Yes Brain Kids: Teach Your Kids About Balance

Derek wanted to play Little League, but he was afraid.

His parents encouraged him, though. They even went with him to the first practice, and his mom volunteered to help coach the team.

The first practice he didn't love it, but the second practice was pretty fun. Then, in his first game he got a hit, and it turned out he had a blast. Now he loves baseball. And he wouldn't have known that if he hadn't been willing to confront his fear and try something new.

Yes Brain Kids: Teach Your Kids About Balance

Do you ever feel nervous like Derek did about playing baseball? Do you ever feel pulled a little bit into the red zone, or maybe into the blue?

It's not easy to be brave, especially when you feel yourself outside the green zone. But sometimes, when you try something new, you find out you can do more than you realize.

It feels really great to be brave when something is hard. Plus, it will make your green zone even bigger, and you won't miss out on new experiences you might really enjoy! You learn that you can do hard things, and that feeling uncomfortable or afraid is okay and that you can do it anyway!

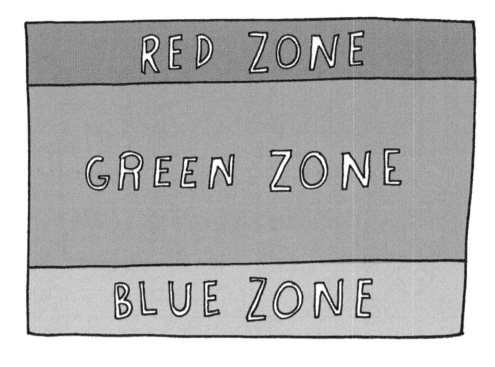

MY OWN YES BRAIN: PROMOTING RESILIENCE IN MYSELF

Now that you've given so much thought to developing resilience in your kids, let's turn the attention back to you. The more you work on building your own Yes Brain, the better you'll be able to support your kids as they build theirs. Next is a series of questions to help you reflect on your own resilience and how developed your Yes Brain is.

Have you ever noticed a pattern in terms of what sends you out of the green zone? In other words, are there certain triggers, or circumstances, or a particular state of mind (overwhelmed, confused, angry, etc.), that can send you to either the red or blue zone? Take a minute to think on that and write your thoughts here:

What is the experience like for you to actually be in the red or blue zone—emotionally (anger, fear, etc.), physically (heart beating fast, tense muscles, etc.), behaviorally (yelling, shutting down and refusing to talk, etc.)? How long do you tend to stay there?

_____

_____

_____

_____

When you're in the red or blue zone, what have you found to be the most effective way to return to the green zone? Do you take a break? Listen to music? Take a walk? Different people have different tactics for making this internal reconnection happen, to bring themselves back to the green zone. What's yours? Also, is there anything that helps keep you in the green zone (like enough sleep, etc.)?

_____

_____

_____

_____

What are your "growth edges," or the particular areas that need strengthening in your resilience resources? For example, Are there specific situations that are especially challenging? Is moving back to green when you've been in the blue or red difficult to achieve? Is monitoring your internal world to reveal signs of leaving the green zone for the rigid blue zone or the chaotic red zone something that's challenging at this point in your life? Think about it and write your answers here:

_____

_____

_____

_____

Can you support your own growth and resilience? Resilience can be seen as how readily we can bounce back after a disconnection—in our relationships and within our inner life with emotional distress. Being human means finding ourselves in moments of disconnection. Resilience involves coming back into connection. This might involve seeking some help from friends, relatives, or others when needed, and building your own inner skills of self-regulation for different situations. Take your time and write your thoughts on the lines that follow. If you sense you'll need outside support, write down some specific steps you can take to make sure you have that.

_____

_____

_____

_____

Many of us find the process of building our own resilience challenging. It requires hard work and perseverance. But knowing that building our own Yes Brain, and facing challenges with resilience, is possible, and gets easier with practice. Plus, we'll be modeling that behavior for our kids, which is a great incentive.

CHAPTER 4

Insight

*With insight we don't have to remain helpless in the face of our feelings and circumstances.
We can look at what's going on within our internal landscape and then make conscious,
intentional decisions, rather than blindly following destructive, unconscious impulses.*

—The Yes Brain

Insight, the third Yes Brain fundamental, is something you may not have thought as much about as the others. But it's crucial when it comes to living a life full of meaning, honesty, and self-understanding. Simply put, insight is the ability to look within and understand ourselves, and then use what we learn to be more in control of our emotions and behaviors.

By paying close attention to our inner world, by slowing down and thinking about our reactions and our emotions when they occur, we gain an understanding of why certain events affect us the way they do. With that understanding, we're better able to respond intentionally to circumstances, as opposed to having our lives run by our reaction to stimuli.

As an adult, you may have some insight into why a particular activity frightens you. Or you might be consciously aware that certain circumstances make you feel more secure and happy, while others make you irritable. But to what extent do you help your children understand *their* emotions and motivations? When your child reacts to situations, how often do you help them process the "why" behind the behavior or inside their minds? How often do you help them think about their reactions?

Keep your child's common challenging behaviors in mind when looking through the next set of questions:

1. When my child has returned to the green zone after flipping their lid, I help them understand the motivation for their behavior.

    o Most of the time

    o Occasionally

    o Rarely

2. After my child has had a meltdown, I help them develop insight into the emotions and desires that prompted their behavior.

    o Most of the time

    o Occasionally

    o Rarely

3. When I flip my lid, I model explaining the reasons behind my own behaviors.

    o Most of the time

    o Occasionally

    o Rarely

4. I encourage my child to use language beyond "mad" and "sad" to explain the emotions they feel when leaving the green zone.

    o Most of the time

    o Occasionally

    o Rarely

5. When my child is in the red zone, I'm able to stay mindful that their behavior is communication.

    o Most of the time

    o Occasionally

    o Rarely

6. When I'm entering the red zone, I'm mindful enough to be able to shift my awareness to realize what I'm doing.

    o Most of the time

    o Occasionally

    o Rarely

None of us parent perfectly, and none of us parent perfectly all the time, but what we're asking you to think about is to what extent your radar is tuned in to helping your child develop insight about their emotions and behaviors. If you answered "occasionally" or "rarely" to any of these questions, what do you think you can do to increase your awareness of moments when you could instill this type of understanding in your child?

_____

_____

_____

THE PLAYER AND THE SPECTATOR

Let us teach you a concept about self-observation; then we'll talk about applying it for our kids.

One of the best ways to gain insight is to become an observer of yourself. That means noticing and even embracing the emotions you're feeling in the moment, while simultaneously observing your reactions to those emotions. In other words, you're feeling your feelings in the moment (the player) as well as watching yourself feel those feelings (the spectator).

The key is learning how to pause in the heat of the moment and observe from a place of objectivity. In that moment, there's no judgment being made, no faultfinding, you're just noticing what's going on. And from that place you're better able to make calm, thoughtful choices. We're not saying this is easy. But with practice, you can learn to greatly improve your ability to take control of how you respond in upsetting situations.

As you start to work on having more insight into what's going on in your mind, it's important to remember to keep a patient, kind attitude toward yourself. An aggressive reaction toward thoughts and feelings you think are "bad" is really common, but the goal here is simply noticing — not passing judgment. Different methods for increasing your mindfulness work for different people, but here's one method for getting started:

Begin by setting some time aside to take a slow, leisurely walk without headphones or earbuds. Not a goal-oriented one, but a walk that's just a walk. It doesn't need to be long; even 10 or 15 minutes will do. Busy people tend to find it hard to really slow down to the point where they no longer feel time pressure. But a walk like this can be almost a mini-vacation. Give yourself the luxury to take these few minutes to return to the pace and openness of a child. As you walk, notice what's around you. Sensory awareness is step one to being more tuned in to yourself.

- Turn your focus in to your sensations. Take note of what you hear, what you see, what you smell, what you feel (_physically—the wind in your hair, the pain in your shoulder, and so on_).
- If your mind wanders to something like work or your kids, take notice of that, and then shift your attention back to just being where you are and, once again, what you are seeing, hearing, smelling, and feeling _in the moment_.

The Player and the Spectator

Insight lets you observe yourself so you're not a victim
of your feelings and circumstances

The spectator offers perspective

• After your walk, take a few minutes to journal about your experience. Keep in mind that you aren't trying to make any meaning out of it all; it's just an exercise in noticing (i.e., *when I was walking, I noticed the sound of children talking nearby and cars honking. I was aware that my shoes were a bit tight, and I noticed how warm my body was*). You may want a separate journal if you continue to do this over time, but you can start here:

_____

_____

_____

_____

Next, take time out—either that same day or sometime soon after—to sit still and perform a similar exercise, but this time focus on your *emotions*. Rather than physical sensations of the outside world or from your body, notice your emotional feelings. Don't judge them, don't create meaning, just notice them.

• To begin, find somewhere quiet and comfortable where you can be alone for a few minutes. This type of reflective exercise can be uncomfortable or difficult for people who aren't used to it, so you may want to start with a minute or two and work your way up to longer.

• Become aware of your breathing. There's no special way to breathe. Your body already knows how to do it. Just notice the sensations of the movement of the breath, in and out. You can feel it as a sensation in your nostrils, or as the rising and falling of your abdomen. Then, as you attend to your breathing, you may notice how thoughts and feelings capture your attention so that you lose track of the breathing. That gives you an opportunity to get to know your inner experience of your mind—your feelings and thoughts and sensations—more intimately. For this exercise, you'll be focusing on emotions.

• As you sit, take note of what emotions you feel (*This is irritation. I'm aware of sadness*). Now, take note of your reactions to your emotions—these may be bodily sensations or thoughts such as: *My shoulders tensed when I started to feel angry. I had the thought that I don't deserve to feel happy.* Remember, whatever thoughts you have are simply thoughts. No thoughts are wrong. There's no need for judgment. There's no need to reprimand or praise yourself. You're just noticing, being open to whatever arises in awareness.

- When you're done with the time you've set for yourself, take another few minutes to journal about the experience. What did you notice? Again, you'll continue to do this over time, so you may prefer to start in a separate journal. If not, write your thoughts here:

_____

_____

_____

Often, in a reflective exercise, sometimes called a "meditation," at first you'll feel as though you're paying deliberate attention to your feelings and noting them in a conscious, pointed way. With a little practice, this will feel effortless. By practicing these suggestions on a regular basis, you're setting an intention to be mindful. Mindful awareness entails an open, receptive state of mind—coming with what Dan calls a COAL state of being curious, open, accepting, and loving. In being more mindful, you become better able to respond thoughtfully and consciously, instead of reactively. As you continue to do this, you create new neural pathways so that this way of thinking starts to come naturally when it's needed. This is how the intentional creation of a state during a practice becomes an automatic trait during the rest of your life. There's a quality of spaciousness and freedom that develops from this kind of contemplation. You're a little less "caught up" in your feelings and preoccupations. You've given yourself literal breathing space, and that allows your innate wisdom to respond with patience and resourcefulness to situations as they arise.

You can try a more elaborate exercise at Dan's website: DrDanSiegel.com, and explore the Wheel of Awareness. In his book, *Aware*, you'll find a step-by-step guide to the practice and science of being more present in your life. In the Wheel metaphor for the mind, the rim is what we are aware of, and the hub is the experience of being aware itself. The hub represents the spaciousness of being mindful, of pausing before reacting, of having that COAL state of receptivity. It is with this presence that as parents we can support the four S's of our children to enable them to become securely attached to us.

THE POWER IN THE PAUSE

One thing that keeps us from developing or using our insight is, again, reactivity. Instead of being receptive, we can feel threatened and become reactive. Too often we experience a stimulus and immediately react rather remaining receptive and flexible.

The Genesis of a Meltdown

But if we can pause, instead of reacting and letting the situation send us into the blue zone or red zone, we have a much greater chance of maintaining control over ourselves.

Then we can bypass the immediate reaction and give ourselves a better chance of remaining in the green zone.

What happens for many of us is that we react to triggers in an instinctual way that make us uncomfortable—often resulting in lashing out, or other maladaptive behaviors, as a way to avoid the discomfort. For example, your child talks back to you, you feel disrespected, which feels unpleasant, you react to that unpleasant feeling by reprimanding your child for their behavior as a way to get rid of your discomfort. Now you've created a rupture with your child, you haven't actually solved the issue of their behavior, and while you may be momentarily better, you're also training yourself to avoid your feelings.

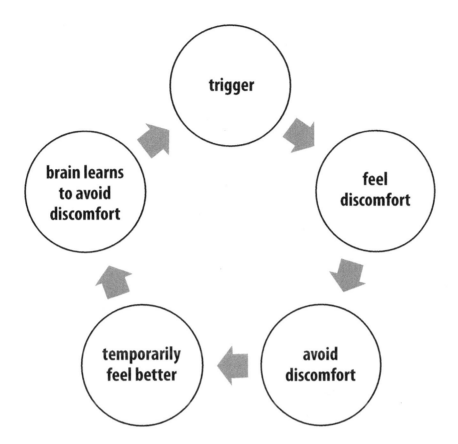

Part of what happens as you practice your mindfulness is that you become more aware of your bodily sensations and your internal sensations that are activated in response to stimuli. This awareness is a first step toward being able to pause when triggered. Using the previous example, your child talks back to you, you feel disrespected, you feel discomfort in your body, you pause (maybe taking a breath to help calm you down, or by stepping away from an argument). From there, you can label your feeling (i.e., *"This is shame"*) and ask yourself where it comes from or why you feel that way (if you know, but if you don't, just put a pin in it and consider it at a later time). This can be called "name it to tame it." The pause and the labeling lets you calm down and respond thoughtfully to your child in a way that allows you to get your point across so that they hear you, as opposed to creating a reactive moment in your child.

The more you practice this pausing, the more easily it comes to you when you need it. The more curious you become about your reactions, the more you become able to separate them from the trigger that sparks them so you can choose how you want to respond. You're literally retraining your brain to know that experiencing your feelings actually helps you feel better.

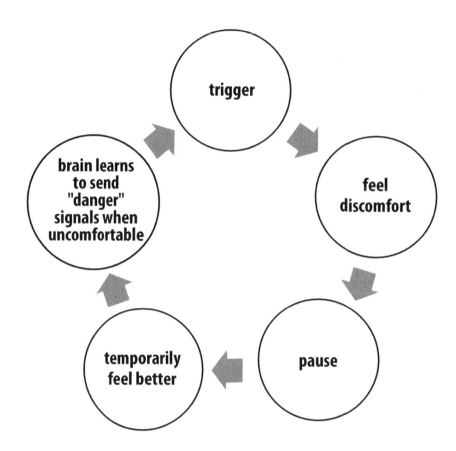

So, now that you're working on being more mindful, let's try practicing the pause. For some people, being able to pause in the heat of an argument may feel like an impossibility, so let's start with something less stressful.

Begin this exercise by focusing on something small that tends to irritate or upset you (*no one replaced the toilet paper roll, your son didn't make his bed in the morning, the corner coffee shop is out of your favorite muffin, etc.*). The next time something like this aggravates you, stop and pay attention to your reaction. Don't judge it as being the "right" or "wrong" response; just notice what you're feeling and thinking and what happens from there. Bring that COAL state of receptive awareness to whatever is going on.

You can detail your own experiences with practicing your pause in the following table. In particular, think about how you've reacted in the past and what results you got, compared with what results you got when you paused before responding. We provided an example to get you started.

TRIGGER	REACTION	OLD RESULT	NEW RESULT
Late for work. Slow traffic.	I started to get really angry and then panicked because I would be even later. Then I remembered to pause. I took a deep breath and just noticed how my body felt and the thoughts I was having.	Usually I would get more tense, sometimes yelling in my car. Or driving recklessly to get around the slower cars. My body would be stiff and tense. By the time I got to my office I would be angry and impatient.	I noticed that when I paused, instead of building on the angry thoughts, they just passed. I became aware of the tension leaving my body and even though the cars weren't moving any faster, I felt less stressed and could think logically. I called my office and told them I would be a little late, and everything was fine.

As you continue to practice this skill, it will become clear how much you can change your experiences just by shifting the way you think. Then, once you feel confident with it, you can teach it to your kids!

Take a minute to imagine how different your children's lives could be if they learned now how to pause and make insightful choices when they face challenges! As they grow into teens and young adults, imagine how much more calmly and lovingly they'll be able to parent their own kids. By helping develop insight and response flexibility in your kids when they're young, you can lay a foundation for literal generations of emotional and relational success.

What You Can Do: Yes Brain Strategies That Promote Insight

Yes Brain Strategy #1 for Promoting an Insightful Brain — Reframe Pain

Any mature adult understands that pain and struggles can often be good for us. This is the awareness that the spectator brings to a situation that the in-the-moment player may not have. Our children, however, don't have the advantage that years of experience bring to us.

This first strategy focuses on helping kids develop a perspective based on an understanding that life is often difficult, and that rather than always expecting to get their way, we can help them ask the question, *"Which struggle do you prefer?"* In other words, teaching your child to reframe a difficult situation in such a way that they recognize each option they have presents its own challenge, but ultimately, they get to *choose* which path to take. Your child being able to pause and look at a situation with "spectator vision" allows for choice in how they respond, for meaning to be created out of these tough experiences, and for increased confidence in handling what life throws at them.

If you look at the chart that follows, you can see an example of a struggle a child might have—feeling that they don't have any friends. In order to get what they want, they have two options (for the sake of this example), and each of those options has a risk and a payoff. When your child is able to reframe the pain of feeling friendless, and look at their situation without an emotional attachment to a particular outcome, they can weigh the options and make a logical decision about what their next step will be.

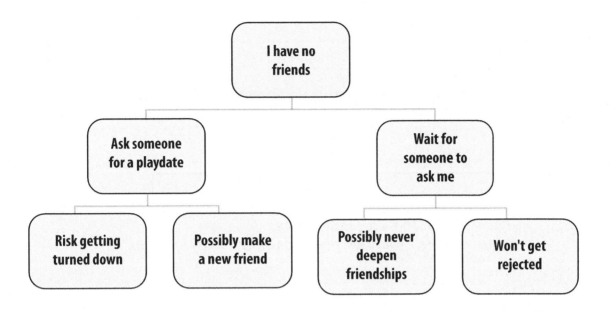

Let's practice this with challenges your own child is facing. We've started this exercise off with an example of a struggle a child may potentially have. You can see that in the first section we listed the challenge. In the second section we've reframed the pain and broken it down into choices. And in the third section, you can see how they chose to solve this situation. After reading through it, think about struggles that are specific to your own kids; consider how you can reframe the pain for them; and then—together with your child—support them through choosing which sacrifice they're most comfortable with in order to solve their problem.

Example

Challenge

- *My coach never picks me to be the starting pitcher.*

Reframe

- *If I want to pitch, I have to practice more.*
- *If I practice more, I'll have less time to do other things I like to do.*

Solution

- *Playing baseball is my favorite activity and if I want to be really good at it, I have to devote more time to it.*
- *I'm better at it than I am at soccer, so for now I will focus on one sport.*

Challenge 1

Reframe

Solution

Challenge 2

Reframe

Solution

Challenge 3

Reframe

Solution

With practice, our kids will be able to reframe unwanted or stressful experiences into neutral or even positive ones. They won't be able to control everything that happens to them, but over time they'll learn to pause before reacting, become aware of what they're feeling, and then choose how they want to respond.

Yes Brain Strategy #2 for Promoting an Insightful Brain—Avoid the Red Volcano Eruption

You'll remember from *The Yes Brain* that the Red Volcano is about hyperarousal—when we become upset about something, the arousal of our nervous system increases. We feel it in our bodies: our heart beats faster, our breathing increases, our muscles get tense. As we become more and more upset, we move up the bell curve (or, up to the top of the Red Volcano). This is where the danger lies. As we get to the top of the curve, we enter the red zone and explode, losing our ability to control our emotions, decisions, and behavior.

The Red Volcano

Eventually, we come down the other side of the mountain and enter the green zone again, but it'd be preferable to never actually hit that point where we lose control and erupt. The key to this is to be more aware of what sets you (and your kids) off, and what signs you give that you're inching your way up the volcano.

Let's begin this exercise by focusing on something that frequently upsets you (*something to do with your kids, something at work, etc.*). Remember, it doesn't have to just be anger. Emotions such as anxiety, fear, and stress can also set us off.

- Fill in the first section of the chart that follows with the trigger you choose.
- In the next column, list any warning signs you see that your sympathetic nervous system is becoming hyperaroused—in other words, what signs are indicating that the volcano is heating up and beginning to rumble.
- Then, in the last column, show what insight could intervene and stop the process. What steps could you take to help cool things down? As usual, we've started you off with an example.

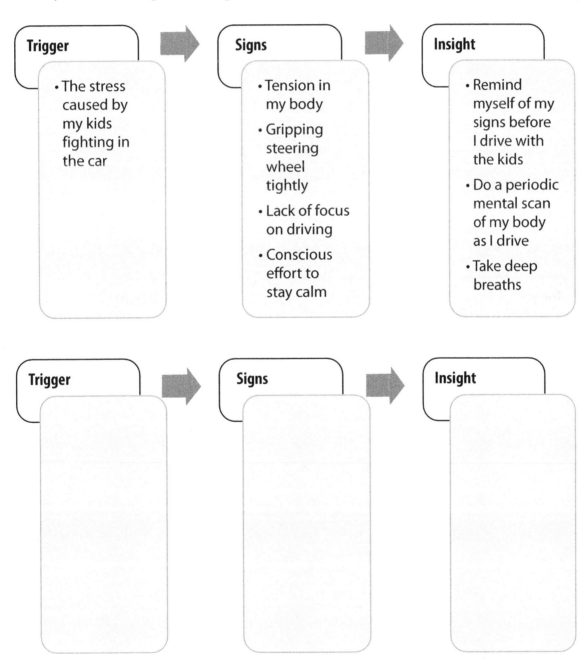

Trigger
- The stress caused by my kids fighting in the car

Signs
- Tension in my body
- Gripping steering wheel tightly
- Lack of focus on driving
- Conscious effort to stay calm

Insight
- Remind myself of my signs before I drive with the kids
- Do a periodic mental scan of my body as I drive
- Take deep breaths

Trigger

Signs

Insight

After you've done one for yourself, choose a trigger that frequently sets your child off (*school, siblings, sports, etc.*) and go through the same process as you did previously.

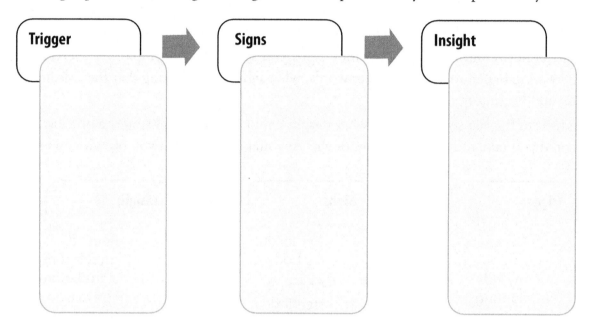

Continue to work through additional triggers for both you and your children.

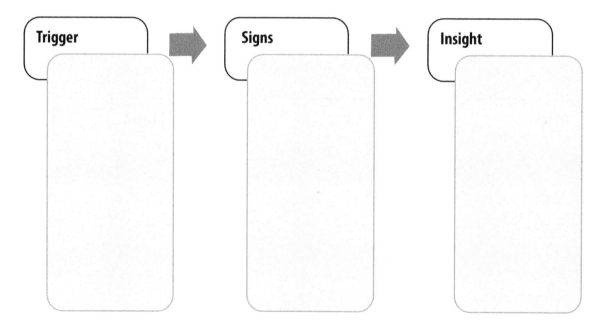

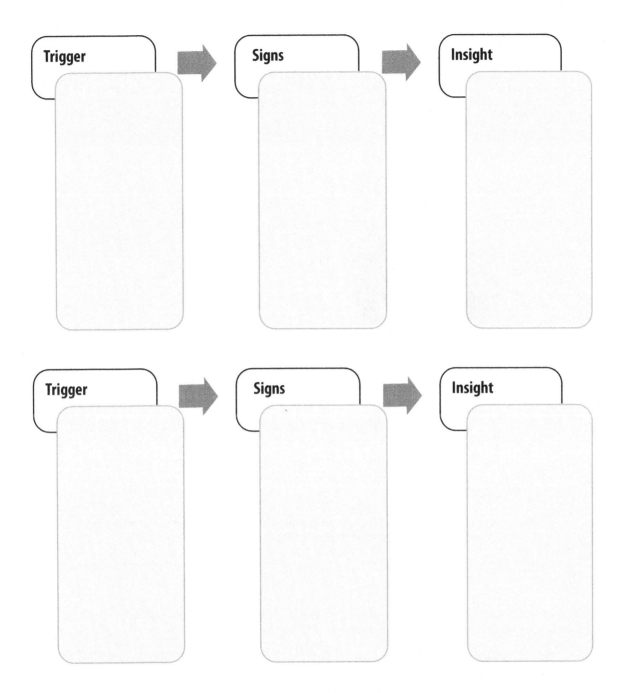

The point of doing this is to learn to think ahead, so that you're ready to pause when necessary, and so you have some clear and specific steps you can take to help bring yourself (and your child) back into the green zone. Doing this with your child obviously helps you understand their signals so you can help them avoid getting triggered any further and, ultimately, teach them how to work through the process for themselves.

YES BRAIN KIDS: TEACH YOUR KIDS ABOUT INSIGHT

On the following pages we've provided a Yes Brain Kids (YBK) series you can read with your child to help introduce this idea, and to help them think about it in the future.

Yes Brain Kids

Let's talk about your feelings again, and focus on the red zone, and what you can do to avoid going into the red zone in the first place. Think about your feelings as a volcano. As long as you're down low on the mountain, you're in the green zone. You feel peaceful and calm.

But when your feelings start getting really big and you get upset, you start up the mountain, toward the red zone. And guess what happens when you reach the top? You erupt!

That might mean yelling at someone, throwing an object, tearing something up, or just totally losing control.

There's nothing wrong with getting upset. But what if we could keep from reaching the top of the red volcano? What if we could catch ourselves when we began to get upset, and not ever erupt? Wouldn't it be better if we just paused and took a breath?

This is what happened with Brody. His brother, Kyle, threw a ball that hit him in the eye, and Brody was so mad! He wanted to throw something at Kyle, or say something really mean to get back at him.

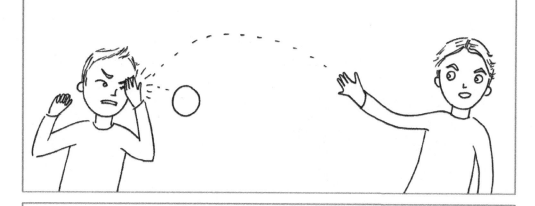

But instead, he paused and took a deep breath. This is the key. He thought about the red volcano, and he made himself pause. He was still furious—just as mad as before. But he didn't act on those feelings.

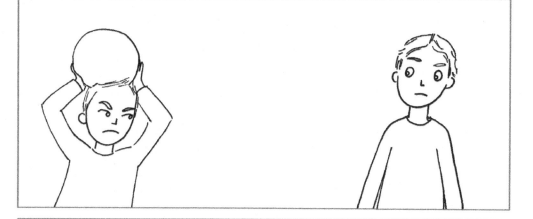

That's all you have to do when you feel yourself moving into the red zone: just pause. You don't have to stop being upset. Just pause before erupting. Then you can take a moment and think of a different response, like asking your parents for help, or telling someone how you feel.

MY OWN YES BRAIN: PROMOTING INSIGHT IN MYSELF

One of the most important skills to learn (for anyone) is the ability to notice when your own anger, frustration, or fear, is escalating so much that you're moving out of the green zone. One key sign is when your reaction isn't proportional to the offense (i.e., *you flip your lid because your child broke a plate, you fall apart when your kids don't listen to you, or you panic at the idea of being late*). When we develop insight into our memories and how the past influences us in the present, we become able to respond with intention, as opposed to being driven by habit and emotion.

With that in mind, this is a good time to take a look at your own childhood and your experiences with your parents or caregivers so you can think about and develop a coherent narrative regarding your experiences. Here you will see a few questions to spend some time with. Consider how your experiences have affected the way you think and respond and behave in the present day.

What was it like growing up in your house? *(What were your economic circumstances? If you had siblings, what were your relationships like? What was the neighborhood and community like? How were holidays celebrated?)*

_____

_____

_____

_____

What memories do you have of your parents/caregivers? *(If you had regular conflict with them, what was it over? How was it generally resolved? Did your family support you and your interests? How involved in your life were your parents? How did your relationship with them change as you grew older?)*

_____

_____

_____

_____

How was school for you? What did you like about it? What was hard for you?

_____

_____

_____

_____

When you think about your present-day triggers, do you see any connections to your childhood/ early life? *(As an only child, I'm used to being alone and in a quiet house. Now, as an adult, the chaos that comes with having multiple children is hard for me to handle.)*

_____

_____

_____

_____

What do you know of your own parents' childhoods? How do you think their upbringing affected the way they parented you and your siblings?

_____

_____

_____

_____

After reflecting on these questions, in what ways do you think your childhood experiences affect your parenting?

_____

_____

_____

_____

Obviously, childhood challenges and experiences of trauma or loss can be incredibly impactful in shaping someone's development and worldview. But sometimes, even the smallest events make a big impact. It's important to look at your memories from the point of view of the child who was experiencing these moments and consider how the adult you are now can help make sense of them. Being able to create a coherent narrative about our childhood experiences enables us to have more compassion for ourselves, to better understand our strengths and stretches, and to be able to make more conscious decisions about how we live our lives.

CHAPTER 5

Empathy

If parents can combine their empathy with the insight we discussed in the last chapter,
the resulting mindsight will allow them to be more patient and receptive and understanding and aware,
which will let them enjoy deeper and more meaningful relationships, and be happier overall.

—*The Yes Brain*

As we pointed out in the previous chapter, cultivating personal insight, with an awareness that allows us to maintain clarity regarding our own motivations, emotions, and desires, helps us focus on living out of a Yes Brain. Going hand-in-hand with insight is the quality of empathy, which allows us to remain aware of and join with the experiences of others. Combined, insight and empathy offer the building blocks of Mindsight.

What's great about empathy is that, like balance, resilience, and insight, it can be learned and practiced. We tell a story at the beginning of Chapter 4 of *Yes Brain* about a boy whose parents worried that he was born completely bereft of empathy. But with their help, and the continued practice they offered him at developing this important relational quality, he became a teenager who was able to think about others and even sacrifice his own desires in a healthy way when necessary.

In this chapter we want to help you learn to offer your own kids this same gift. The gift of developing empathy within themselves.

An Opening Question: Is My Child Too Selfish?

Do you ever worry that your child demonstrates too many selfish traits? Do any of these characteristics sound familiar?

- Doesn't share
- Insensitive to others' feelings
- Resists doing chores
- Has to be bribed or rewarded for basic good behavior
- Doesn't apologize
- Manipulates to get what they want
- Greedy
- Jealous
- Never satisfied/always wants more
- Lack of gratitude
- Lack of interest in others
- Disregard for other people's time
- Disinterest in helping others
- Always puts their own needs first
- Brags
- Self-absorbed
- Self-centered

Let's start by breaking down those behaviors that concern you about your individual kids, remembering that behavior is communication. In the first column of the chart that follows, list any selfish behaviors you think your child exhibits. In the next column, write down what concerns you have about the fact that your child is behaving that way. In the last column, consider whether you think it's possible that some patience is required because the behavior is developmentally appropriate. And finally, write down what your plan of action will be to work on this issue. We provided a couple of examples to give you an idea of what this might look like.

BEHAVIOR	CONCERN	CAUSE
• Doesn't share her things.	• She is self-centered and I worry she isn't considering others and that other kids won't want to be friends with her.	• She hasn't learned to share yet. • She hasn't had practice yet.

My Plan:

Be patient because most of it is probably developmental. She still needs to learn how to consider others' feelings and to share—I don't want to budge on that—but maybe I can start with asking her if she can choose a toy to share for a few minutes instead of waiting until a moment when someone tries to take a toy away. Then I can affirm her for being a good friend.

BEHAVIOR	CONCERN	CAUSE
• He's always trying to have everyone's attention on him. • He makes everything about himself.	• If he keeps doing it he won't have friends. and people won't like him. • People will think he's rude. • People will think I'm a bad parent.	• He's four, so probably it's developmental. • He hasn't learned yet that he's not the center of everyone's focus. • He's enjoying showing off his new skills and abilities.

My Plan:

I need to remember that when he interrupts, and tries to get the focus on himself, that he hasn't yet learned to see things from any other point of view. I'll gently remind him that someone else is talking or that it's someone else's turn and explain how his behavior makes people feel. Over time he'll learn. I need to remember that his behavior isn't a direct reflection on me as a parent.

BEHAVIOR	CONCERN	CAUSE

My Plan:

BEHAVIOR	CONCERN	CAUSE

My Plan:

BEHAVIOR	CONCERN	CAUSE
My Plan:		

Now let's take a look at what's been going on for your kids that might possibly contribute to what you see as their current self-absorbed behavior. We provided some examples of challenges kids may face that can affect their behavior beyond the ordinary developmental changes.

- **School** (*teachers, grades, tests, attendance, performance pressure, etc.*)
- **Health** (*illness, puberty, teething, growth spurt, mental health, insomnia, etc.*)
- **Friends** (*losing them, making them, bullying, teasing, fights, gossip, peer pressure, being left out, miscommunication, etc.*)
- **Family** (*death, divorce, illness, births, fights, estrangement, disconnection, marriage, etc.*)
- **World at Large** (*world news, current events, local events, fear of "bad guys," politics, etc.*)
- **Personal** (*crushes, sexuality, jealousy, negative self-talk, body image, identity formation, etc.*)

As you look back at any selfish behavior you've noticed in your kids that stands out as unusual, can you pinpoint any shifts in their environment that might have contributed to them seeming more self-absorbed? What needs are they trying to get met? Use the column on the left to fill in the behaviors that cause your concern. Then, on the right, fill in any events that may have been going on around the same time that might have affected your kids and their behavior. Once you've done that, make some notes about any action you feel would be helpful (*talking to school counselors, meeting with a doctor, talking to your child, etc.*).

BEHAVIOR	EVENTS

My Plan:

BEHAVIOR	EVENTS

My Plan:

BEHAVIOR	EVENTS

My Plan:

BEHAVIOR	EVENTS

My Plan:

Ultimately, all behavior is communication—whether your child is telling you that there are skills they need help building, or showing you that they're having a hard time processing something that's happening in their life. At times like this, instead of panicking, think about what their behavior is telling you about your child's life and well-being. This way, you can be there to support them in successfully making it through whatever they're struggling with. Even if the behavior is a sign of something that needs some type of outside intervention, you're better able to respond with helpful suggestions when you're calm and collected as opposed to reactive and fearful.

Behavior is Communication

The behavior we see:

What's really being communicated:

BUILDING A BRAIN THAT'S WIRED TO CARE

It's possible that being empathetic is a behavior you don't give much thought to in your daily life, simply because it's something that's become your general way of being. This is a good thing since it turns out that one of the most effective ways of building empathy in our kids is to model it ourselves. Talking about empathy and other people's perspective is important, but when you model it yourself, you really SNAG your kids' brains for empathy.

Stimulate

Neuronal

Activation and

Growth

Let's start this exercise by writing down the ways you model empathy for your kids: (the way you speak to people who are helping you or providing you a service, the time you spend on community service, the way you treat your partner or friends, times you express interest in people around you, etc.). How are you showing your kids that empathy matters to you?

_____

_____

_____

_____

_____

_____

How do you talk about the idea of empathy with your kids: asking about how other people feel, talking about reactions of characters on TV or in a book, discussing current events and how they affect people locally as well as globally, etc.?

_____

_____

_____

_____

_____

_____

How do you think your kids see you when it comes to the way you show your compassion for other people?

_____

_____

_____

_____

_____

_____

What, if anything, would you like to improve in your day-to-day expression of empathy and compassion—either, toward yourself or toward others?

_____

_____

_____

_____

_____

_____

The more we draw our kids' attention to the needs of the people around them, the more it activates their neurons and strengthens the connections in the social networks of their brains. These networks include making maps of the inner mental states of others—what can simply be called "Mindsight maps." When we give them the type of experiences that draw their attention to other perspectives, we SNAG their brains for empathy—including feeling the feelings of others for resonance, perspective-taking, and empathic understanding.

Here are some ways, beyond modeling, you can help build empathy in your kids:

- Draw awareness to characters' emotions and motivations or internal experiences/goals/feelings (when reading, watching TV/movies together)
- Encourage talking about feelings
- Speculate about why someone reacted the way they did (both in real life as well as through media)
- Point out nonverbal cues and facial expressions that help you understand how others feel
- Hold family meetings where you take the perspective of other family members
- Listen carefully to your child's views/encourage them to listen carefully to others
- Ask about their friends and peers, and ask them to be curious about their friends' motivations or needs
- Discuss ethical dilemmas like world problems, but also personal conflicts in their own lives
- Get them involved in charity work or community projects
- Have them participate in chores around the house, and explain that all members of the family work together to help each other out—the idea of many hands making for lighter work.
- Help them see the connection between their actions and the reactions of others, how when they help someone (like opening the door for someone with a stroller or carrying packages) that it is kind and helps them and makes them have a better day.

Make some notes here about anything you think you'd like to try with your kids, and what steps you need to take in order to have that happen:

_____

_____

_____

_____

_____

_____

_____

Empathy is a Yes Brain skill, and a caring brain can be built

Aside from teaching explicitly about it, the other key that can move a child toward empathy is to let him experience his own negative emotions. Again, the point of parenting isn't to help kids avoid pain. Instead, it's about being with them and giving them skills that help them deal with difficult obstacles as they come up. Yes, letting our children struggle and sit in difficult emotions like anger, disappointment, and worry, while we provide support and presence, can be difficult. But it's essential to allow our children to experience the full range of emotions so they can know what it's like for others who feel those emotions. Allowing kids to experience challenges helps them develop empathy for others who are dealing with difficult times.

How good are you at allowing your child to experience negative emotions? Do you frequently send the message, either implicitly or explicitly, that kids should be happy all the time? Do you tend to jump in to immediately distract or fix things or tell them not to feel those emotions? Do you say, "Stop crying," or, "Don't worry," instead of, "I'm here with you while you're sad"?

Let's take a look at how you would respond to a typical struggle your child might have. We provided a couple of examples. After you read through them, fill in the first section with a struggle your child has experienced and what, if anything, you could have improved about your response to it. If they have a current struggle, take a minute to think about the best way to respond to it with this new perspective.

STRUGGLE	RESPONSE
At the end of the birthday party, one of my twins was very sad because his sister had gotten "better" dress-up costumes.	*My first instinct was to buy him the same costume, or to insist they share. But I think if I instead sat with him and let him feel his sadness and frustration that her costumes were more "fun," they both could have learned something about jealousy and accepting what you have instead of wanting something "better."*
My daughter has a tendency to procrastinate when it comes to doing her homework and then gets very upset the night before it's due.	*Because I want her not to be upset and not to get a bad grade, I'm usually nagging her or helping her finish. But I think it would be better to help her create a work schedule and support her when she experiences the consequences of not finishing work in time.*

WHAT YOU CAN DO: YES BRAIN STRATEGIES THAT PROMOTE EMPATHY

Yes Brain Strategy #1 for Promoting a Caring Brain—Fine-Tune the "Empathy Radar"

Your child's brain has what you might think of as an empathy radar. It allows them to read the emotions of others. When it's well-tuned, the radar can help them relate to others on a deeper and more meaningful level. Being well-tuned also means that kids are able to differentiate and use their minds autonomously so they're not hyper-attuned (which can be exhausting) or dependent on others' perceptions for their happiness (which can be paralyzing).

Think for a moment right now about how effective your child's empathy radar is. Using the scale that follows each question, rate how well your child does with each scenario. After each question, write down at least one example that illustrates your opinion.

1. Able to take the perspective of others

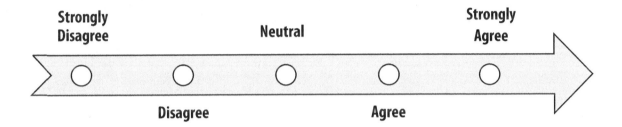

Example:

_____

_____

_____

_____

2. Works collaboratively with others

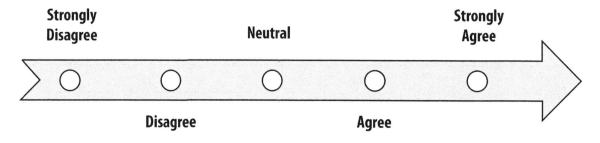

Example:

_____

_____

_____

_____

3. Stands up for others

Example:

_____

_____

_____

_____

4. Able to read nonverbal cues

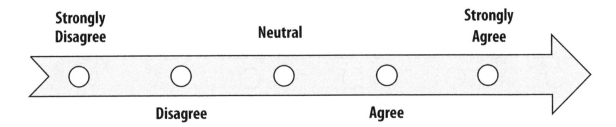

Example:

_____

_____

_____

_____

5. Able to talk about their own feelings

Example:

_____

_____

_____

_____

6. Has compassion for others

Strongly Disagree　　　　　**Neutral**　　　　　**Strongly Agree**

Disagree　　　　　**Agree**

Example:

_____

_____

_____

_____

7. Able to verbalize others' feelings

Strongly Disagree　　　　　**Neutral**　　　　　**Strongly Agree**

Disagree　　　　　**Agree**

Example:

_____

_____

_____

_____

8.   Is a good listener

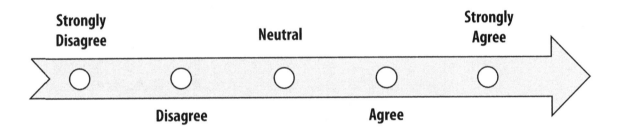

Example:

_____

_____

_____

_____

9.   Voluntarily offers to help

**Strongly
Disagree**   **Neutral**   **Strongly
Agree**

Disagree   **Agree**

Example:

_____

_____

_____

_____

10. Is able to be empathic while still retaining independence

Strongly Disagree   **Neutral**   **Strongly Agree**

○   ○   ○   ○   ○

Disagree   **Agree**

Example:

_____

_____

_____

_____

We can help kids turn on their empathy radars in many ways. One way is to help them see a situation from a place of curiosity, as opposed to one of judgment.

Engage the Empathy Radar

Instead of judging ...

Teach kids to use their curiosity

This curiosity can then lead kids to reframe situations and see them from a more empathetic perspective. One way to do this is through role-play. You'll remember from *The Yes Brain* that we used the example of a boy angry at a friend for cheating at a game. When the parent suggested they role-play and had the boy step into his friend's shoes, he had to imagine *why* the friend was cheating. By doing this he was able to take a different point of view of the situation and have more compassion for his friend.

Think of some recent situations your kids have been involved in that you could reframe by using role-play. Take a minute to write down some examples and, once you've tried it, take some notes on what the outcome was. We provided an example.

EVENT	REFRAME	OUTCOME
My daughter is upset with a friend who constantly copies everything she does (hobbies, clothing, interests, etc.).	Role-play an interaction between child and friend—I will be my child, and she will be her friend.	By doing this type of role-play, my daughter was able to imagine that her friend looks up to her and is trying to be like her, as opposed to "copying" her. She became aware that her friend has a hard time voicing her own opinions, so maybe she feels safer following my daughter's lead. My daughter still doesn't like it, but she understands in a new way.

Fostering the idea of looking at possible motivations behind someone else's behavior helps your child create more understanding, forgiveness, and patience for other people. Sometimes, the best way to encourage this sort of sensitivity is simply to bring attention to where others need support. This can be a serious conversation about empathy, but your everyday interactions will also offer many opportunities to model thoughtfulness.

For example, birthdays and other holidays are a perfect excuse to encourage your kids to think about other people's desires. It's much easier at times to just give a gift card, but thoughtful gift giving is really about tuning into the mind of the other person, and giving careful thought to a good gift for them helps build the empathy muscles. Let's take a look at some ways you can use this idea with your own kids.

Since gift giving is a chance to say something about how well you know someone and how much they mean to you, it can sometimes feel a little daunting. Being mindful about what you know about this person and what you've experienced with them is one way to come up with some ideas for what you'd like to give someone as a gift.

Start by thinking about the person your kids want to give a gift to. Have them help you make a list of what they know about that person. Ask questions that make them think. What hobbies do they have? What do they do for work? What stores do they like to shop at? How did you meet? Have there been any big events you've shared together? What do you know about their past? If they're on social media, what do they post about? Do they have any charities or causes they are active with? Are there any secrets you share that could inspire a gift? Write everything down that you come up with.

_____

_____

_____

_____

_____

Next, think about what gifts from the past you remember them really loving. What have you noticed really makes them the happiest? Not everyone feels seen by receiving a physical gift. Some people prefer an experience or a gift of spending time together. Others will be more touched by words, so perhaps your bookish best friend would love it if you wrote a story about the first time you met and how much she means to you. Maybe you've noticed that one parent feels really overwhelmed by having to work and take care of the house, so a gift of action (like surprising her by coordinating with the other parent or another adult friend to do all the grocery shopping for the week) would make them really happy. Think about the person you're wanting to give a gift to, take a look at the chart that follows, and determine how you think they receive love.

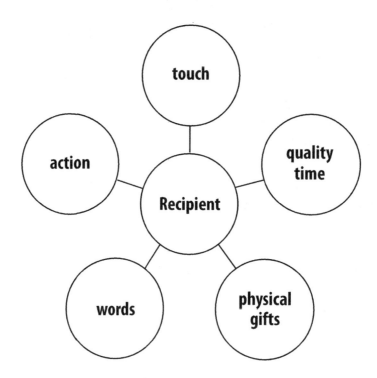

Now you have a list of things you know about your person, and you have a pretty clear idea about what type of gift makes them feel most loved. This gives you a pretty good direction in which to go when you're choosing what to do for them. The chart that follows will help you lay it all out and help you make some decisions. We started you off with a couple of examples to make it easier.

NAME	WHAT I KNOW	TYPE	GIFT IDEAS
Grandma	• Loves flowers • Loves good food • Wishes she could have more time with us	She always says spending time with us is when she's happiest, so, quality time	We'll cut some flowers from the yard and make a picnic lunch for the park, where we can go for a walk
Tutor	• Works long days • Lives alone • Loves her dog • Recently diagnosed with arthritis	The arthritis pain has made her very uncomfortable and she's had to see less clients because of that, so I think maybe action would be most appreciated	• Make her a few meals to take home to keep in the freezer • Buy her a can opener that's easier for arthritic hands • Invite her to bring her dog over for tutoring sessions so you can help play with the dog to give it some exercise

Remember, gift giving is really about showing how much you care about someone. Letting them know that you really see them, that you really listen to them, and that you really understand them is more important than how much money you spend.

Yes Brain Strategy #2 for Promoting a Caring Brain — Establish a Language of Empathy

Teaching kids how to *talk about* empathy is one more way to help them know how to care about others. Even if your kids can take the perspective of others, that doesn't mean they automatically know how to talk about it.

Using "I statements" helps your child understand their own role in a conflict, while also lessening the possibility of defensiveness from the other person involved.

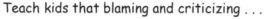
Teach kids that blaming and criticizing . . .

Causes more problems than 'speaking from the I'

Kids also need to learn the art of showing support without immediately telling the other person how to solve their problems. Empathy is much more about listening, being present, and sharing feelings.

So, how do we teach our kids to notice when others are hurting and show them how to respond in caring ways? Phrases like "That must really hurt" or "I'm sorry you feel so sad today" let people know that we're listening, we're being present, and we're trying to show that we're connected.

Teach kids that giving advice . . .

Isn't as powerful as listening and being present

Let's think about ways to help your kids with these skills. Begin by choosing a TV program or movie to watch together with your kids. Afterward, each of you pick a scene that will allow you to talk about how the characters could have responded with more empathy. You can use a separate piece of paper, or the space that follows, to record your thoughts.

Character and scene:

_____

_____

_____

_____

I would change the dialogue this way to have the characters show more empathy:

_____

_____

_____

_____

Character and scene:

_____

_____

_____

_____

I would change the dialogue this way to have the characters show more empathy:

_____

_____

_____

_____

Character and scene:

_____

_____

_____

_____

I would change the dialogue this way to have the characters show more empathy:

_____

_____

_____

_____

Once you've done this a few times, take moments in your kids' own lives where relationships have required empathy (such as moments with friends, grandparents, other children at the playground, etc.), and have your kids go through the same process of talking it through with more empathy. This could include moments of conflict, or situations that required more understanding and compassion. Remember, there are several components to empathy that can come out in these discussions: emotional resonance—feeling others' feelings but not becoming overidentified with them; perspective-taking—seeing through the eyes of another; empathic understanding—cognitively making sense of others' experiences across time; empathic joy—being happy about another's success and well-being; and empathic concern—feeling another's suffering and wanting to compassionately help them to feel better. Again, you can use separate sheets of paper, or use the space that follows to write out your answers.

Situation:

_____

_____

_____

_____

If I'd responded this way, it would have shown more empathy:

_____

_____

_____

_____

Situation:

_____

_____

_____

_____

If I'd responded this way, it would have shown more empathy:

_____

_____

_____

_____

Situation:

_____

_____

_____

_____

If I'd responded this way, it would have shown more empathy:

_____

_____

_____

_____

While studies have shown that children as young as 10 months old have demonstrated the *capacity* for empathy, being able to use empathic language and respond in a way that shows understanding and compassion is something that's learned over time and with practice.

Yes Brain Strategy #3 for Promoting a Caring Brain—Expand the Circle of Concern

When we talk about the idea of building a caring brain, most people's thoughts go to their immediate circle of family, friends, coworkers, and so on. While it's important to consider the needs and feelings of those people closest to us, it's just as important to expand the "circle of concern" to include caring for those we don't yet know and love.

How wide is your child's circle of concern? Do you worry sometimes that your kids are growing up in a self-contained bubble? Let's turn our attention to those questions now.

Who is in your child's circle of concern?

_____

_____

_____

_____

Are there any people included, or left out of, your child's circle that surprise you?

_____

_____

_____

_____

Why do you think those people are, or are not, included?

_____

_____

_____

_____

Now, let's think about ways that you can widen that circle. We provided some examples in _The Yes Brain_, like offering to shovel your neighbors' sidewalks when it snows, or volunteering at a retirement center, or even just signing up for activities that would allow them to interact with kids from various and diverse communities and neighborhoods.

What are some small ways you can encourage your kids to think beyond their immediate circle of concern? We know a mother who made a Kindness Tree to encourage her young children to do just this. She made a large tree out of butcher paper that she hung on the dining room wall, and each day she would ask her kids to tell her at least one kind act they did for different people (the school custodian, the mail carrier, the barista at the local coffee shop).

She then wrote their acts of kindness on a paper "leaf" and attached it to the branches of the tree. Once the tree was filled, they celebrated Kindness Day with a special outing.

Here are some other simple ways you can expose your kids to new ways of being empathetic:

- Read books about kindness.
- Ask your kids to make a list of the people who work at their school, and write down what they appreciate about each one. Create homemade cards of appreciation to give to those people.
- Write notes of kindness and leave them inside books in your local library for people to find—you never know who might need a pick-me-up!
- Challenge your kids to complete three acts of kindness a week, or notice five acts of kindness from others.
- Look up World Kindness Day activities and choose some of those to try.
- Find an international pen pal. There are organizations who will pair your child with kids around the world (often in developing countries)—just make sure you vet the program first.
- Teach your children about "bucket filling" and how doing kind things for others not only makes that person feel good (fills their bucket), but also fills your child's bucket so they feel good as well. Full buckets = happy people = more kindness going out into the world. Then challenge your kids to find someone who might need their bucket filled—it can be something as small as offering a cold drink to the sanitation workers who come by each week, or spending some time making care kits for the homeless in your area.
- When you teach your children about saving money, also talk to them about sharing a portion with charity. This opens a window to help them verbalize what global issues may be important to them. (Do you want a charity that helps children? One that helps animals? Or maybe one that works to help the environment?)

What other ideas can you brainstorm with your kids? You can take some notes here while you do this:

_____

_____

_____

_____

_____

_____

Yes Brain Kids: Teach Your Kids About Empathy

You and your kids can read through the following "Yes Brain Kids" section as you teach them about considering what other people are experiencing.

Yes Brain Kids: In the other "Yes Brain Kids" sections we've talked a lot about paying attention to your own reactions, and what's going inside you. Now we want to talk about seeing what's going on inside someone else.

When you look at a friend, you can see what she looks like on the outside. And if you have an X-ray, you can see the inside of her body.

But did you know you can look at someone with your heart, too? That happens when you notice how that person is feeling, like whether she's happy, or sad, or angry, or excited.

When you use your heart to look at someone, you pay attention to his face, but also his body. Can you tell how this boy feels, just from looking at his body language?

That's Carter. And if you said he looks sad, you're right. He's sad because a bigger boy at school was mean to him and pushed him down.

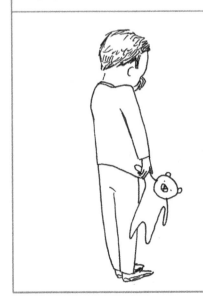

Carter never told Lottie he was sad, but when she looked with her heart, she could tell. She could see her brother's feelings, and her heart hurt.

Since she had looked at her brother with her heart, Lottie knew she needed to check on him. She asked about his feelings, and the two kids decided to ask their mom for advice about the bully.

The next time someone around you is hurting, look with your heart. Pay attention to what that person is feeling. If you can just notice what's going on inside that other person, you'll probably know just what to do.

MY OWN YES BRAIN: PROMOTING EMPATHY IN MYSELF

For many people, self-compassion is a difficult type of empathy to cultivate. Because you're working on modeling compassion for your children, you're working on increasing your capacity for empathy in yourself. One important part of doing this is cultivating empathy *for* yourself.

Next you'll see some questions asking you to take a look at how compassionate you are toward yourself. Take a few minutes with this exercise and tune in to how you think about and treat yourself.

Think about a specific time when you got angry at yourself about making a mistake. What was your self-talk like in that moment?

_____

_____

_____

_____

How often do you find yourself being really critical of yourself? Are there certain moments that bring that out more often?

_____

_____

_____

_____

How much time in your day do you set aside to take care of your mind and body? Do you think you need more? If so, how can you achieve this?

_____

_____

_____

_____

What holds you back from being more compassionate toward yourself?

_____

_____

_____

_____

How understanding are you toward the parts of yourself that you don't like?

_____

_____

_____

_____

When you're going through a hard time, how do you tend to talk to yourself? (Do you keep your emotions in balance? Do you fixate on what's wrong?)

_____

_____

_____

_____

You can compare having empathy for yourself with how you might talk to your best friend. If they were struggling, we're pretty sure you'd be caring and supportive. You'd listen without judgment, and you'd express understanding for how difficult life can be sometimes. If your friend made a mistake, you might even say something like, "Oh, that's something I did, too," or, "That's just what people do sometimes."

Take a few minutes now to think about the moments you detailed previously where you were hard on yourself, times you made a mistake, moments where you weren't your best self. Think about any scenarios where you did something or behaved in a way you're not proud of. Write each one down in the boxes that follow. Then, in the space that follows each box, write a response to yourself using the sort of voice you'd use if your best friend behaved the way you had. We provided you with an example.

Scenario
I offered an opinion in a meeting that everyone criticized.

Response to myself
I'm so proud of you for speaking up. That idea was something you felt strongly about. I know it can be really hard for you to hold a different opinion from the rest of the group, but you did it anyway. Just because other people didn't agree doesn't mean your idea was a bad one. It's Ok to stand out. It's OK to be noticed.

Scenario

Response to myself

Scenario

Response to myself

Scenario

Response to myself

Scenario

Response to myself

The empathy we're trying to teach our kids is the same thing we want to offer ourselves when we make mistakes. And when we do that, we not only help ourselves, we also model this important skill of self-compassion for our children.

CHAPTER 6

Conclusion

How do we help kids develop authentic, intrinsically based success in life? It begins with acknowledging and honoring each child for who he or she is. Every single child has an inner spark—a combination of a unique temperament and various experiences—and we want to fan that flame to help kids become happy, healthy, and internally driven to be the "best them" they can become.

—The Yes Brain

RETHINKING SUCCESS: A YES BRAIN PERSPECTIVE

There's a saying that goes, "There are a thousand ways to be successful, but each of us has to find our own." While this might be something many parents would agree with in theory, when it actually comes to following through with our own kids, the idea of trusting that our children will find their own way when it comes to success might make us feel impatient, or even fearful. The definition of "success" that most of the world holds is pretty rigid, is narrowly focused on achievement, and the idea of veering off that path can be frightening. There is nothing wrong with achievement. We're proud when our kids do well. The gold stars children earn are things we can celebrate, but they are not all that success is about. In fact, they're not even evidence of a child being happy or fulfilled—or having a Yes Brain. And too often, parents, in their efforts to have their kids earn these stars, end up putting the family on the treadmill of success.

The Treadmill of Success

The competition and societal pressures many parents struggle with often cause them to accept ideas that supposedly "ensure success" for their kids that have more to do with their own future-thinking fears and anxiety than with what they know about their children or even what they know about life through their own experiences.

When you ask parents what they want most for their kids, many of them start off by saying something along the lines of, "I just want them to be happy." But does happiness mean the same thing to your child as it does to you? Does success, as it's defined by most of society, equate to happiness? The only way to really know is to help your child find their *own* way to be successful—and that might mean letting them step off the treadmill in order to help them find out who they are and what they're passionate about.

ARE YOU STOKING YOUR CHILD'S INNER FIRE?

Let's conclude with some questions from the book that can help you get clear on what ways you're stoking your child's inner fire, and where you might be verging too close to the treadmill. Take your time to really think about these questions, then write your answers in the spaces that follow.

Am I helping my kids discover who they are and who they want to be?

_____
_____
_____
_____
_____
_____

Do the activities they participate in protect and promote their individual inner sparks? Do these activities contribute to the development of balance, resilience, insight, and empathy?

_____
_____
_____
_____
_____
_____

What about our family calendar? Have I left room for them to experience moments where they can learn and explore and imagine, or do we go at such a frantic pace that they never get to relax, play, be curious, create, and just be kids?

_____
_____
_____
_____
_____

Am I emphasizing grades and achievement more than I should? Or am I pushing my child into something that's more about me than about them?

_____
_____
_____
_____
_____
_____

Am I communicating to my children that what they do is more important than who they are?

_____

_____

_____

_____

_____

_____

Is my relationship with my child being eroded by my constant pushing for them to do more or be better?

_____

_____

_____

_____

_____

_____

In the way I communicate with my kids, am I helping their individual sparks grow, or am I diminishing them?

_____

_____

_____

_____

_____

_____

What we spend our money and our time on, and what we argue about with our kids, can often reveal a lot about what's really important to us, and it can reflect what our children think matters the most to us. So, we want to work on being aware of how we may, even subtly, be at odds with our own goal of helping kids think for themselves, be empathic, discover their passions, and be proud of who they are.

Helping kids develop a Yes Brain, then, comes down to two primary objectives:

1. Allowing each individual child to grow into the fullness of who he or she is, as opposed to imposing our own needs, desires, and designs.
2. Watching for times our child needs help with skill-building and developing the tools necessary to thrive.

Guiding our children as we watch them grow into people who know who they are, are able to face challenges with resilience, can trust their instincts, and who treat others with kindness and compassion is one of the great joys of parenting. In giving them the gift of a Yes Brain, we set them up for the chance to live rich, full lives and to have truly authentic success.

Acknowledgments

We appreciate all the parents, grandparents, coaches, educators, clinicians, and others, who have read and recommended our books through the years. We also want to thank PESI for being so supportive throughout the whole publication process. We especially appreciate Karsyn Morse and Linda Jackson, our editors. They have supported us for years in various capacities of our relationship with their press, and we love working with them. And finally, and as always, we want to thank Gina Osher, who has once again played a huge role in the creation of this workbook. We are grateful for the time, energy, and insight she has generously offered.

About the Authors

Daniel J. Siegel, MD is a clinical professor of psychiatry at the David Geffen School of Medicine at UCLA, the founding co-director of the UCLA Mindful Awareness Research Center, and the executive director of the Mindsight Institute. A graduate of Harvard Medical School, Dr. Siegel is the author of several books, including the *New York Times* bestsellers *Aware* and *Brainstorm*, and is the co-author with Tina Payne Bryson of *The Whole-Brain Child, No-Drama Discipline, The Yes Brain,* and *The Power of Showing Up*. He lives in Los Angeles with his wife, with welcome visits from their adult son and daughter.

Tina Payne Bryson, PhD, is the co-author (with Dan Siegel) of two *New York Times* bestsellers—*The Whole-Brain Child* and *No-Drama Discipline*—each of which has been translated into dozens of languages, as well as *The Yes Brain, The Power of Showing Up,* and the upcoming *The Bottom Line for Baby*. She is the Founder and Executive Director of The Center for Connection, a multidisciplinary clinical practice in Southern California. Dr. Bryson keynotes conferences and conducts workshops for parents, educators, and clinicians all over the world, and she frequently consults with schools, businesses, and other organizations. An LCSW, Tina is a graduate of Baylor University with a Ph.D. from the University of Southern California.

Made in the USA
Las Vegas, NV
02 November 2022